THE DIAMOND DUST

Anil Kumar Srivastava
Akshay Srivastava

Qurate
quratebooks.com

THE DIAMOND DUST
Anil Kumar Srivastava & Akshay Srivastava

Published in 2025

© Published by

Qurate Books Pvt. Ltd.
Goa 403523, India
www.quratebooks.com
Tel: 1800-210-6527, Email: info@quratebooks.com

ISBN: 978-93-58984-23-1

Introduction

The Ramayana is the **spiritual constitution of Sanatan Dharma** in India. While it may be easy to write moral lessons in a book, it is far more difficult to live by them. This is why, when the purity of **Satya Yuga** began to decline, **Lord Vishnu** incarnated in human form as **Lord Rama**. He faced nearly every possible difficulty and hardship in life, yet never adopted any unethical practices or thoughts. This was because **Lord Vishnu had to live the principles he was laying down** in the spiritual constitution of Sanatan Dharma. No one should ever say it is impossible—because even a prince lived through the harshest trials with unwavering righteousness.

The Ramayana contains the answers to all of life's questions. Whatever your situation may be, when you read the Ramayana, you will find a solution within it.

In this book, various chapters present real-life challenges and how the Ramayana provides a path forward. The purpose of this book is to offer guidance—especially during times when you may not have an elder or mentor to advise you. Books, however, are always there to guide you.

Some people raise questions due to a lack of clarity on certain issues. That's why, in the following age, **Dwapar Yuga**, Lord Vishnu again incarnated—as **Lord Krishna**—to provide deeper guidance on dealing with even more complex and unethical situations. This further clarity was offered through the **Bhagavad Gita**.

Building on these foundations, **the Constitution of India** was eventually written, which addresses every aspect of life and ensures the opportunity for justice in all circumstances.

Storybooks may bring momentary joy, but in order to live a meaningful life, **our youth must engage with profound and serious literature**. They are the future of India, and books are the lamps that illuminate the path in times of darkness.

Anil Kumar Srivastava, Author
Akshay Srivastava, Co-Author

Contents

CHAPTER - 1

Morning And Night Prayers - Cosmic Wisdom

Hindu Dharma teaches that if we pray either early in the morning or before going to sleep, our prayers are considered by God. There is a deep science behind this belief.

At night, just before we fall asleep, our conscious mind begins transferring all the accumulated data of the day to our subconscious mind. While we sleep, the conscious mind repairs the body, and the subconscious mind connects with universal forces to recharge the body's energy.

In the morning, the subconscious mind transfers this renewed energy and information back to the conscious mind. During these two transitions—falling asleep and waking up—both the conscious and subconscious minds are simultaneously active and connected to the universe. That is why prayers made during these moments are quickly received and honored by cosmic forces.

No one is aware of the exact moments when we shift from active to sleep mode or return from sleep to active consciousness. These transitions are controlled by cosmic command, beyond human control. The cosmic wisdom directs us to sleep so that the necessary repairs can be made to the body and the daily data can be uploaded and restored.

This is clear proof that there are cosmic forces actively managing our lives and well-being.

****

CHAPTER - 2

84 Kosi Ki Parikrama

Vaidic and Sanatan Dharma have a profound understanding of cosmic science and its relationship to the human body. All Vaidic celebrations are rooted in cosmic effects and align with the universe's natural rhythms.

The human body itself is a microcosm of the universe. Every human body is equivalent to 84 finger-widths in size. This measurement is based on a calculation where the width of four fingers, multiplied and divided by 21 (a divine figure), represents a unit of the body. Scientifically, the body is said to be created from the energy of 252 kilometers (84 miles or kos).

The soil power of 252 kilometers is considered divine. The number 9, a sacred figure in Vedic science, governs this measurement, as any number added to 9 results in the same sum (e.g., 9 + 1 = 10, 1 + 0 = 1). It is believed that a healthy human body can circumambulate 252 kilometers in 40 days. This measurement serves as a parameter for gauging physical fitness. Completing such a journey is said to imbue the body with the strength of the land's soil.

The tradition of the 84 Kosi Parikrama has often been misunderstood. While it is associated with traversing villages around Ayodhya or Mathura, the essence lies in a cosmic connection. Bowing to the divine and maintaining a healthy body is equivalent to circling the entire universe. When you care for your body, you harness the power of the 252-kilometer soil.

As I have highlighted in my other writings on Hindu festivals, these celebrations often symbolize different cosmic events. Similarly, the 84 Kosi Parikrama is a cosmic phenomenon.

Dharma is, in fact, astronomical science. The festivals were created as a way to honor and remember various cosmic events, ensuring their eternal significance.

****

CHAPTER - 3

The Voice Of Washerwoman

The Ramayan serves as the foundational constitution of India, its principles deeply embedded in the ethical and moral fabric of society. The present Indian Constitution follows a similar pattern, emphasizing justice, duty, and the importance of public voice in governance.

One of the most profound examples of righteous governance in the Ramayan is Lord Ram's decision to consider the voice of a washerwoman who doubted Goddess Sita's purity, despite her having already undergone the Agni Pariksha (trial by fire). This was not an act of personal doubt but rather a profound message for future rulers, emphasizing that a king must govern in a manner where every voice, no matter how small, is heard and respected.

The Devas (celestial beings) descended from the universe with a divine purpose that is to teach humanity the ideals of righteousness and duty. At a time when human civilization viewed deities as beings of unattainable power, Lord Vishnu chose to be born as a human to exemplify the responsibilities of a good king, son, husband, and leader. Ram's life was a blueprint for human conduct, offering lessons in governance, sacrifice, and justice.

Lord Ram, along with his divine companions, ultimately returned to the celestial realms. Goddess Sita merged with the earth, while Bharat and Shatrughna entered the sacred waters of the Sarayu River. Their mortal remains were never found, reinforcing their divine origins. They were composed of god particles that dissolved into pure energy, beyond the grasp of human existence.

The Ramayan's teachings offer a roadmap to an ethical life, emphasizing:-

- Education for all: Just as Ram and Laxman studied in the Gurukul like common students, education remains the foundation of a just society.
- Respect for parental authority: The duty to honour one's parents, as Ram upheld his father's promise without hesitation.
- Service over power: True leadership is about responsibility, not ruling for personal gain.
- Valor and righteousness: Courage should be used to eliminate evil, as seen in Ram's battle against Ravan.
- Equality for all: Ram's unwavering love for Shabri, Nishadraj, and Hanuman demonstrated that caste and status hold no value before genuine devotion and virtue.
- The power of technology: The construction of the Ram Setu with advanced engineering techniques proves that progress lies in action, not blind worship.

The Ramayan provides solutions to every challenge of human life. No situation exists for which an answer is not found in its verses.

India's Constitution is deeply influenced by the Ramayan's principles of justice, equality, and governance. Just as Ram upheld duty above all, every citizen has the responsibility to protect, honour, and seek guidance from the Constitution, ensuring a society based on ethical governance and collective well-being.

Lord Ram's life serves as a timeless guide for individuals and leaders alike. The Ramayan is not just a story—it is a manual for righteous living. By embracing its teachings, society can build a future that upholds justice, duty, and honour, preserving the ethical values that have guided India for centuries.

Do not read the Ramayana as religion book or a as story of Ram. It's a constitution of human civilization. A guide to live a pure and meaningful life on earth.

****

CHAPTER - 4

Vibhishan Should Be Worshiped

Vibhishan, the brother of Ravan, left the golden kingdom Lanka because he chose righteousness over material wealth. It is incorrect to say that he went against his brother; rather, he opposed his brother's wrongful policies and character. This was his ultimate test in life—whether to stay in a golden kingdom built on injustice or to uphold righteousness. His correct decision to stand with Ram ultimately made him the ruler of Lanka, without even desiring it. This is how cosmic power maintains justice.

Praying to God while having a polluted heart and character will never yield true blessings. Cosmic wisdom recognizes what lies within, beyond mere physical actions. These divine forces are connected to our minds and hearts, not just our hands and bodies.

There are clear messages for human civilization—to stand with righteousness like Ram stand with Kewat, Nishad, Shabri, and Sugreev. Ram followed this path by uniting all good forces to defeat evil, cleansing the earth of destructive thoughts and powers.

Ramayana has endless hidden messages. Never read it as religious books. Read it like human constitution on earth.

****

CHAPTER - 5

Melt The Gun And Make Toys

In this chapter I invite you to reflect on a very simple yet powerful sentence:-

"Melt the gun and make toys - this is how we can save the earth."

This isn't just a poetic phrase. It is a call for humanity to shift from destruction to creation, from war to peace, from fear to love.

Across the world, we see nations spending trillions on weapons - creating arms not to protect, but to dominate. Guns, missiles, and bombs have become symbols of power. Yet ironically, they are also symbols of fear, insecurity, and destruction. What have we achieved? Wars, refugee crises, hatred, and a planet drenched in sorrow.

Now contrast this with a toy in the hands of a child. A toy does not harm. It brings a smile, sparks creativity, and fills life with joy and innocence. A toy represents imagination, learning, and play - the very foundation of a peaceful society. If our factories melted the steel of weapons and forged it into toys, swings, bicycles, and bookshelves instead - imagine the message we would be sending to the next generation.

The world doesn't need more weapons. It needs:

- Schools, not bunkers.
- Books, not bullets.

- Doctors, not soldiers.
- Love, not war.

By melting guns and making toys, we are choosing to invest in the future of children rather than the politics of destruction.

The universe, as many ancient scriptures say, responds to our intentions and vibrations. When we build weapons, we attract fear. When we build love and innocence, the universe aligns with us. It is not just our political responsibility, but also our cosmic responsibility to make the earth a safe and nurturing place for all.

To the leaders of nations: channel your budgets from defense to development.

To the youth of this world: reject violence, embrace innovation, and be the change-makers of peace.

So, what can we do?

- Let us raise our voice against violence.
- Support disarmament movements.
- Teach children the power of compassion.
- And most importantly, start by creating peace within ourselves.

Melt the gun. Make a toy. Give a child a future.

This is not just a dream – it is a necessity if we truly wish to save the earth.

****

CHAPTER - 6

God Lives In Purity

God is always connected with our pineal gland—the spiritual antenna within us—and knows the purity and depth of our devotion. When the heart is pure, and faith is unwavering, the divine does not need an invitation; He simply arrives.

In the age of Satya Yuga, when young Prahlad called upon the Lord, God appeared from a mere pillar. In Treta Yuga, Shabari waited with utmost devotion, and Lord Ram walked through forests just to meet her. In Dwapar Yuga, Draupadi cried out in despair in the Kuru assembly, and Krishna came instantly to protect her.

Even today, God listens. Perhaps He has already come to you many times—in forms you did not recognize, in situations that seemed ordinary, or through people you may have ignored. Why do we fail to see Him? Because we have created an image of God that is fixed and limited. We look for Him in idols, temples, or rituals, forgetting that He resides in truth, in love, and in purity of intention.

Those who are not pure, who live selfishly and engage in unrighteous actions, often rush to temples and beg from God—pleading for money, success, or long life. But the divine does not respond to demands that come from ego and entitlement. The universe gives not what we desire, but what we deserve.

First, we must become deserving. We must purify our minds, align with truth, and serve selflessly. When we walk the righteous path, God

Himself walks toward us. When we remember Him with sincerity, we do not need a temple. No structure of stone can substitute the temple of the heart.

True devotion does not require rituals or offerings. It requires purity of soul, clarity of thought, and unwavering faith. Those who truly love God can feel His presence anytime, anywhere—because God does not live in temples alone. He lives in the soul of the pure.

****

CHAPTER - 7

The Heinous Crime

One of the most tragic and heinous crimes in the history of civilization has been the treatment of widows, especially in India. For centuries, widows have been treated as second-class citizens—excluded from auspicious ceremonies, stigmatized in society, and deprived of basic human dignity. In many parts of the country, even today, a widow is seen as a bearer of misfortune, unworthy of participating in celebrations or holy rituals.

This cruel mindset stands in stark contrast to the teachings of Sanatan Dharma, whose true constitution is the Ramayana. The Ramayana is not just a scripture; it is a divine demonstration, where Lord Ram himself lived every role—of a son, a king, a husband, a brother—and provided guidance on how one should navigate life, especially during times of great moral challenges.

One of the most powerful and often ignored messages of Ramayana is the right of a widow to remarry and live a dignified life. After the death of Ravan, Lord Ram instructed his brother Vibhishan to marry Ravan's widow, Mandodari. This was not just an act of compassion but a clear constitutional directive: marriage is not merely about companionship—it is also a sacred duty to protect and honour a woman's life.

Yet, history took a dark turn. Long before the Mughal era, a cruel tradition emerged—Sati, where widows were burned alive on the funeral pyres of their husbands. It was the most inhumane act imaginable: to punish a grieving woman with death. Many people try to shift the blame to the Mughal period, claiming that widows were unsafe. But the truth is this—Sanatan Dharma had already offered a divine solution: the right to remarry, to live, and to be protected.

Unfortunately, cowardly custodians of religion ignored Lord Ram's teachings. They justified violence and cruelty under the guise of culture and custom. They forgot that true followers of Lord Ram must uphold his principles—not just chant his name.

Even today, widowhood carries a social stigma. Many refuse to marry a widow, treating her as inauspicious. This is not just a social failure; it is a spiritual failure. India must recognize this black spot in its civilizational journey—the historic and systemic injustice against widows.

If followers of Sanatan Dharma genuinely adhere to the principles laid down by Lord Ram in Ramayana, and further illuminated by Lord Krishna in the Bhagavad Gita, they will not only restore justice to women but also reclaim their place as a spiritual leader in the world. Because to be close to God, one must first be just, compassionate, and courageous.

****

CHAPTER - 8

Forgive And Forget

The Ramayana is not just an epic—it is the spiritual constitution of Sanatan Dharma. At its heart lies a message that has the power to transform human relationships and society as a whole: "Forgive and Forget."

Throughout The Ramayana, Lord Ram faced many situations where hatred, revenge, or bitterness would have been natural responses. Yet, time and again, he chose the path of forgiveness and compassion. These divine choices are not just stories—they are lessons for humanity.

1. Forgiving Mother Kaikeyi

Queen Kaikeyi, under the influence of her maid, demanded that Lord Ram be exiled for 14 years, clearing the path for her son Bharat to ascend the throne. Despite this betrayal, Lord Ram bore no hatred toward her. Instead, he displayed the highest form of humility and respect for his elders. His forgiveness not only preserved family unity but also transformed Kaikeyi's heart, leading her to regret her actions deeply. This is the power of forgiveness—to melt even the hardest of hearts.

2. Forgiving Sugreev

After Lord Ram helped Sugreev reclaim his kingdom by defeating Bali—Sugreev's own brother who had wrongfully usurped the throne and taken his wife—Sugreev initially forgot his promise to help Ram search for Sita. Rather than punishing Sugreev or expressing anger, Ram chose to wait and forgive. This kindness awakened Sugreev's conscience, and he went on to become one of Ram's strongest allies in the war against Ravan.

3. Offering Peace to Ravan

Even when Ravan committed the most unforgivable act—kidnapping Sita, Lord Ram extended a hand of peace. He sent Angad to Ravan's court, offering him a chance to return Sita and avoid war. Ram did not seek bloodshed, even when it was justified. His actions showed a clear desire to save lives, including those of his enemies. Only when Ravan refused did Ram take up arms, proving that forgiveness comes first—but justice must prevail when evil persists.

4. The Lesson from the Ocean God

Before crossing to Lanka, Lord Ram prayed for three days to the King of the Sea, humbly requesting safe passage. When his prayers went unanswered, Ram prepared to take forceful action. Only then did the sea god surrender, seeking forgiveness. True to his nature, Ram forgave him and made him an ally. This incident shows that firm action becomes necessary only when humility is ignored, and even then, forgiveness remains the higher ideal.

The Path Forward for Humanity

The Ramayana teaches us that a humble and compassionate heart is the key to peace—both within and in society. If we truly followed these divine guidelines, the world would be a more forgiving, united, and harmonious place. But today, we are moving away from these values, and our civilization suffers as a result.

Forgiveness is not weakness. It is divine strength. When forgiveness fails to reform, only then must action be taken—but even action must be rooted in justice, not hatred.

Until we embrace the principles given by Lord Ram, we will continue to wander in conflict. The time has come to reawaken our spiritual wisdom—to forgive, to forget, and to live with humility and grace.

****

CHAPTER - 9

Life Is Examination Room

Once upon a time, in the vast tapestry of existence, it became evident that divine beings, even those graced with godly power, had to undergo the most rigorous trials to prove their worthiness. These trials weren't reserved for ordinary mortals alone but extended even to the avatars of supreme gods. This is the tale of such trials—of Lord Ram and Lord Krishna, whose lives were tests scripted by the cosmic will.

In the golden age of Treta Yuga, Lord Vishnu incarnated as Lord Ram, a beacon of righteousness. Born into royalty, Ram's destiny seemed to promise a life of prosperity. Yet, the night before his coronation as king of Ayodhya, a twist of fate plunged him into exile. Stripped of the comforts of royalty, he was commanded to live as a hermit in the wilderness for 14 years. Alongside him were his devoted wife, Sita, and his loyal brother, Lakshman.

The journey was anything but serene. Ram faced demons, wild beasts, and treacherous paths. His resolve was tested time and again, from resisting temptation to the ultimate challenge—rescuing Sita from the clutches of the demon king Ravana. Ram emerged victorious, not merely because of his divine powers, but because of his unwavering adherence to duty, justice, and compassion. It was his endurance, even in suffering, that elevated him to be worshipped as God, revered for millennia.

Then came Lord Krishna, the playful yet profound incarnation of Vishnu, in Dvapara Yuga. His life began in turmoil, born in prison under the shadow of death. His tyrannical uncle, King Kansa, sought to kill him even before his first cry echoed in the dark cell. Krishna was smuggled to safety and grew up in the humble village of Gokul. As a child, he lived among cowherds, often tending cattle and playing his flute, all while evading numerous assassination attempts by Kansa.

Krishna's life was a testament to enduring trials. He battled evil forces, moved his people from Mathura to Dwarka for their safety, and faced the devastating war of Kurukshetra, where family fought against family. Despite his divine wisdom, Krishna experienced heartbreak, loss, and betrayal. In the end, his own people succumbed to internal strife, leading to their destruction. Krishna's life concluded with a mortal's fate—struck by an arrow from an unknowing hunter.

These stories of Ram and Krishna hold a timeless lesson. Even those closest to divinity are not spared from the crucible of life's challenges. The gods seem to whisper to humanity through these tales: "Life is not a playground; it is an examination room." Just as the avatars faced their trials, every individual must navigate their own, proving their worth through actions, character, and endurance.

The cosmic truth remains unchanged—no temple rituals or river dips can absolve one of wrongdoing. True redemption comes through purity of heart and sincerity of effort. Hardships, then, are not punishments but divine gifts, shaping and testing the soul.

And so, as we reflect on these sacred tales, let us remember: life's trials are a testament to our potential. The question is not if challenges will come, but how we will rise to meet them.

****

CHAPTER - 10

Birthday

The birthday is an astronomical celebration. When the Earth takes a complete round of the Sun in 365 days, we celebrate that in a difficult universe, our Earth has completed one round of the Sun, whereas every second, there is a risk not only to Earth but to human civilization. We thank those universal forces that are saving us.

Slowly, we forget the real sense of celebrating birthdays and anniversaries. We only know that after a year, we have to celebrate again. But understanding what ONE YEAR signifies is important.

Normally, humans pray for a happy future, but your future will be happy only when the future of Earth will be happy. Refer to my book "Ved - Decoding the Mystery of Universe", where I have quoted the content of the Veda. When aliens, to whom we refer as gods, moved from Earth, they entrusted the safety of the Earth to us. Fire is everywhere—under the Earth, above the Earth, in water, in air, and in the body. When the fire is unhappy with us, we all risk being burned.

So, when you celebrate a birthday or anniversary, it is not only for you; it is for Earth and for all the divine forces that kept us safe for a year, enabling us to complete the Earth's round journey.

Be scientific and be spiritual, because both are science.

****

CHAPTER - 11

Yes, I Am A Father

Once, I was in the depths of the earth, surrounded by soil. There was no air, no atmosphere, no friends, and no light, yet I made myself strong and survived with whatever I had. I found small traces of water to drink, and the soil gave me the strength to grow. Slowly, I emerged from the depths of the soil into the open air. I was weak, surrounded by strong trees with towering trunks. Danger was everywhere, and survival seemed uncertain. But there was a divine presence that gave me trust and hope.

Gradually, I grew and became a full tree. My branches and leaves absorbed air and sunlight, making me stronger each day. I felt immense joy when flowers bloomed on my branches, but the happiest moments were when flowers turned into fruits. I couldn't eat the fruits I bore, but I gave them to those who were hungry. When someone took a fruit from my branches and ate it, I felt profound happiness because the purpose of my life was fulfilled. I realized I existed to bring happiness to others.

Those around me would freely take fruits, and I never stopped them. I felt joy knowing they trusted that I would provide whenever they were in need. I gave them not just fruits but shelter, pure air, and support through my branches.

No, I am not a tree. I am a father who grew through the toughest situations and always provided for my family. I offered them a strong shelter and joy, shielding them from life's hardships, even as I bore the brunt of challenges.

Yes, a day will come when I will grow old. I will have fewer fruits, my branches will be bare, and one day, I will die. But I am content. I have fulfilled my responsibilities in life. I was never unfair to anyone. I never hesitated to share my fruits or pure air. I never reacted angrily when they climbed on my fragile branches, nor did I complain when they threw stones at me to get more fruit.

YES, I AM A FATHER.

I have embraced my role on this earth with happiness and pride.

****

CHAPTER - 12

Cosmic Powers Melt Into Cosmic Elements

The cosmic powers that descend to Earth for a specific purpose—to protect or guide human civilization—always merge back into cosmic elements. They have never been cremated, nor do their graveyards exist.

- Lord Ram ascended to a divine planet aboard the Pushpak Viman.
- Lakshman and others disappeared into deep waters, never to be found again.
- There are no graveyards or funeral records for them.
- No historical records exist for Lav and Kush.
- Lord Krishna built the city of Dwarka, but according to legend, it submerged into deep waters. However, no one knows exactly what happened.
- Goddess Sita returned to the core of the earth.
- No historical records exist for Lord Hanuman.
- There are no records of divine sages such as Saint Dadhichi, Saint Agastya, and Saint Kashyap, among many others.
- No records exist for Rukmini and the other wives of Lord Krishna.
- The Pandavas, along with Draupadi, ascended to heaven, leaving no earthly remains.

It is surprising that history has no records of the families and close ones of these divine beings.

What happened to Mother Kaushalya, Kaikeyi, and Sumitra? What became of the wives of Lakshman, Bharat, and Shatrughan? No one knows.

This proves that human civilization failed to preserve the records of their divine protectors. While human history has been documented, the divine beings who walked among us ultimately dissolved into cosmic elements. In the end, they vanished in such a way that no records remain—only oral traditions and sacred stories passed down through generations.

****

CHAPTER - 13

Cat Race And Rat Race

When a cat chases a rat, most of us would naturally assume the cat will win. After all, the cat is bigger, stronger, and built for the hunt. But surprisingly, in many cases, the rat escapes. Why?

Because the cat is running for a meal—something it wants.

The rat, on the other hand, is running for its life—something it needs.

That difference changes everything.

The cat may be hungry, but the rat is desperate. The cat has a goal, but the rat has no choice. And in that moment, the rat will often run faster, turn sharper, and try harder—because its entire existence depends on it.

This small example carries a powerful lesson for all of us: success doesn't always belong to the strongest, the smartest, or the most resourceful. It often belongs to the one who is most driven.

In life, in business, in personal goals—it's not always about who has the most talent or advantage. It's about who wants it more. It's about how deep your "why" runs. When your purpose becomes a matter of survival—not just success—you'll be surprised at what you're capable of.

So ask yourself today:

- Are you running like the cat—or like the rat?
- Is your dream just something nice to have, or something you must achieve?
- Are you chasing goals with convenience—or with conviction?

The difference between average and extraordinary lies in the intensity of your purpose. The rat wins not because it's faster, but because it is fully committed to the outcome.

So in your journey—run like your life depends on it. Because your future does.

****

CHAPTER - 14

The Widows

The Ramayan serves as the constitution of Sanatan Dharma, offering the best judgments for all situations.

When Ravan was killed, his wife, Mandodari, came to meet Lord Ram. Not only did Ram entrust the entire kingdom of Lanka to Vibhishan, but he also advised him to marry Mandodari. Vibhishan was greatly surprised, as he never expected such a suggestion—after all, Mandodari was his brother's wife. However, marrying a woman is not merely about establishing a family life, it serves a higher purpose—protecting and providing shelter for women, especially widows who have lost everything with the death of their husbands. This is a divine act of duty.

India once had the cruel and inhumane tradition of Sati, where widows were burned alive. Many people, in an act of cowardice, tried to justify it by blaming Mughal rule, claiming widows were at risk and had no alternative but to die. However, such individuals failed to understand the teachings of the Ramayan, which had already provided a clear constitutional guideline—widows have the right to remarriage and protection.

Divine forces have always left a clear message, the first responsibility of humans is to protect the weak and the poor, to help those in need. Ignoring this message and burning a woman alive is one of the greatest crimes ever committed on Earth, and it was so-called Hindus who engaged in this practice. By the grace of God, the British eventually arrived in India and abolished this heinous tradition.

Universal forces always maintain justice and find solutions to human suffering. The cries of burning women shook the cosmic order, compelling divine intervention in the form of the British, who came to save Indian women from such atrocities.

****

CHAPTER - 15

Cosmic Engineering

The human body is a masterpiece of cosmic engineering. It is composed of five cosmic elements: Earth (soil), air, water, fire, and space (sky). Besides these five basic elements that construct our physical body, two essential "software programs" run to make the body operational.

The first software is Intelligence—our brain. The brain is not artificial intelligence; rather, it is pure intelligence. Our eyes, nose, tongue, mouth, ears, hands, and legs all function based on instructions from our intelligence—the mind. Similar to modern AI, the mind informs us about our likes and dislikes. It reads the energy of others and helps us determine whether an unknown person may be good or bad. It warns us, stores our daily experiences as memory, and continuously processes information.

Among the five cosmic elements, space (sky) is unique—it is invisible and pertains to the cosmic realm. Our abilities to smell, hear, and see are influenced by this element.

Additionally, we are owned by God, and the god particle, in the form of the soul, resides within us. The soul is the primary source of divine ownership and never permits us to engage in wrongdoing. It constantly alerts and warns us against unethical actions. However, due to the karma system created by God, we sometimes override the soul's guidance. If we truly listen to the soul, we will refrain from wrongdoings.

Out of the seven elements, three are visible, and four are invisible:

1. Visible elements: Earth, water, fire.
2. Invisible elements: Soul, mind (AI), sky/space and air. These four are the most challenging to understand. Mastering their existence can give us control over life and death.

In the human body, consciousness is the key indicator of life. However, whether it originates from the mind or the heart remains unknown. The human body challenges modern science by revealing that while we are gaining knowledge about the three earthly elements, we are still unaware of the fourth element—space (sky)—which is fundamental to consciousness. The remaining two elements represent the god particle.

Perhaps, our ancient ancestors understood the fourth element of space. This might explain why they could travel in space without a physical body, visit other planets, and even meet Devas, who were, in fact, inhabitants of other planets. For this reason, they were less attached to their physical bodies and instead focused on spiritual growth.

We have real challenge to understand this most understandable human body.

****

CHAPTER - 16

Silver Coating

A silver coating can't change the taste of a sweet; it only looks appealing from a distance. This concept applies to life as well. Many individuals strive to present a polished exterior, yet their internal behavior doesn't align with this outward appearance. From afar, they may seem like gentlemen, but in times of need, their true nature emerges.

This discrepancy is evident in noble professions, such as healthcare. Medical practitioners and institutions often advertise themselves as compassionate, but when truly needed, excessive charges, unnecessary operation, costly medicine and tests can financially devastate individuals. Consequently, people are compelled to obtain medical insurance, as treatment costs have become unaffordable for the average person. Here, humanity falters. If a higher power were to remove us from the earth, eradicating our civilization, we couldn't question the decision; we don't deserve the privilege of human life.

Similarly, in marketing, enhancing a product's appearance can attract initial interest, but it's the inherent quality and value that ensure sustained success. Research indicates that 74% of customers consider product quality the most important factor in maintaining brand loyalty.

Therefore, whether in personal conduct or the business world, genuine humanity is essential.

****

CHAPTER - 17

The Cosmic Composition of Life and Its True Purpose

Human existence is a marvel of cosmic engineering. Our bodies are not mere collections of atoms; they are a harmonious blend of the five fundamental cosmic elements—Earth, Sky, Air, Water, and Fire—coupled with a sixth element: the soul, often likened to a divine or God particle. This intricate combination is not designed for selfish pursuits such as greed, crime, hatred, bribery, or enmity. Rather, it is meant to elevate us, to inspire a life of purpose and meaning that transcends material gain.

At its core, our very existence is a testament to the universal balance of nature. The elements that constitute our physical form are the building blocks of the world around us. Earth provides the stability and structure, while Sky and Air bring movement and life-sustaining breath. Water nourishes and cleanses, and Fire transforms and energizes. When these elements combine within us, they create a vessel of immense potential. But it is the soul—the spark of the divine—that infuses our being with consciousness, morality, and the capacity for compassion.

If we were to misuse this divine combination, embracing negativity and unethical behaviors, we would be squandering the true gift of our creation. Instead of allowing greed and corruption to dictate our actions, we must look beyond the superficial and focus on what truly matters. The real meaning of life is not measured by material accumulation or fleeting successes but by our commitment to serving humanity and walking the righteous path laid down by divine wisdom.

In a world where many chase after wealth and power, the simplest yet most profound act of connecting with the divine is to help those in need. This service to others is not only a moral duty but also a powerful means of tapping into the higher energies within us. By offering assistance without expecting anything in return, we align our actions with the universal laws that govern creation. This selfless behavior nurtures both our soul and the collective well-being of society, reinforcing the balance and harmony intended by our cosmic design.

In essence, our existence is a call to live a life of purpose, characterized by service, compassion, and ethical integrity. When we embrace this higher calling, we honor the divine blueprint from which we were made. We transcend the narrow confines of material pursuits and align ourselves with the eternal principles of love and generosity.

The next time you reflect on your life, remember that you are composed of the very elements that make up the universe—powerful, pure, and divinely ordained. Use this realization as a guiding force to live a life dedicated to the welfare of others. In doing so, you not only fulfill your own potential but also contribute to the creation of a more compassionate and enlightened world.

****

CHAPTER - 18

Real Hero and Reel Hero

The modern civilization is more attracted to reel heroism because without doing anything just from a artificial reel they became famous like hero. This practice is similar to shifting from real to reel. The life is not reel, it is real. When the problem will come, the reel will not work, the real hero will work. When there was terrorist attack on Mumbai, the real hero as NSG came to save Mumbai. The reel industry was hidden in their rooms. Take a seen when Hawaldar Abdul Hameed was alone when the Patton Tanks of Pakistan surrounded him. Abdul Hameed with a simple artillery gun started fighting with them and he made graveyard of Pattan Tanks of Pakistan. These tanks were unbeatable, but beaten by a Hawaldar Rank India Hero. At last a bomb came on his head and he died.

The other incident see when the Freedom Fighter Chandra Shekar Azad was making plan with his friends for freedom ,due to leak of information of his presence, British police captured the whole park. A single brave killed to many , fight bravely and at last one there was last bullet in his Mauser Gun , he shot himself so that he is not in hand of British.

There are endless Hero of War and civil services who have done extra ordinary with bravery and courage. They are the real hero. The reel make people coward. Our youth should not be attracted on artificial scene but to do for country and human civilization. There is no reel go out of earth boundary but the bravery inside soul which reel will be made by your soul only. It will be recorded on database of God.

Be brave and Real Hero not the Reel Hero.

****

CHAPTER - 19

The Diffeence of Content of Energy

In Yajurved, in first Khand at Kandika 17, 7 and others there is difference between energy is given. The major difference is given as under :-

1. The energy which cook the food is mixed with God of Anna hence, is a holy energy.
2. The energy which is used for worry or Chinta is energy which cook the meat. In fact in worry the energy burns our body inside hence, the energy used in worry is energy cooking meat and the energy.
3. The energy which is used for Yajny (Yagya) is a holy energy because it burns the all bad thinking hence it is the purest energy. Due to energy with no bad elements or negativity it goes in universe in fastest mode. This is the reason the Yajny is essential part of life in Hindu Dharma. Our prayers thorugh yagya has fastest way to send our prayers and promises to god.

It is very important to note that in such oldest period our knowledge about cosmic function and its relativity with human was very much aware and had in depth knowledge.

This is very clear message to start to make yagya a daily part of life.

****

CHAPTER - 20

Purushottam Mass - Alighment of Lunar and Solar Year

Purushottam Maas, also known as Adhik Maas or Mal Maas, is a highly significant month in the Hindu calendar that appears only once every few years. In 2020, for instance, this extraordinary month was observed from 18 September until 16 October. This extra month is introduced to balance the discrepancy between the lunar and solar calendars—a practice rooted in ancient astronomical calculations.

Astronomical Foundation

The Hindu lunar calendar is based on cycles that differ from the solar year. While a solar year comprises 365 days and 6 hours, a lunar year is only 354 days long. This difference of approximately 11 days, 1 hour, 31 minutes, and 12 seconds per year accumulates over time. To reconcile this disparity, an extra month—Adhik Maas—is added roughly every 32.5 months (or approximately every 2.7 years), as described in the astronomical system. Unlike the Gregorian leap day, which adds a single day every four years, the Hindu method involves incorporating an entire thirteenth month, making it one of the most precise calendar adjustments in existence.

Spiritual and Religious Significance

Beyond its astronomical importance, Purushottam Maas carries profound spiritual meaning. According to tradition, when this month was established, none of the other deities wished to be worshipped during this rare period. Consequently, they entrusted its veneration solely to Lord Vishnu, which is why Adhik Maas is also known as Purushottam Maas. Devotees are encouraged to observe this holy month through practices such as Shri Prabhu Seva (devotional service), fasting, charitable giving, and other acts of devotion that purify the soul.

So, finally the Purushottam Maas is an exquisite blend of science and spirituality. Its existence underscores the deep astronomical knowledge of ancient sages and reflects a harmonious balance between the cosmic and the divine. As a corrective mechanism to align the lunar and solar years, it reminds us that the universe operates with precision and purpose. More importantly, it calls upon us to devote ourselves to the higher ideals of self-improvement and spiritual enrichment. By engaging in the practices associated with this sacred month, we not only honour our ancient heritage but also pave the way for a more enlightened future.

****

CHAPTER - 21

The Fundamentals of Powerful

In Yajurveda, Chapter 1, Kanda 1, it is written that Lord Sun is the most powerful entity in our solar system, and so he should use his power for development, not for destruction. There is a clear message from the Devas, who were the representatives of God to the entire solar system where we reside: that power should be utilized for creation and development. It is also mentioned in other places that eliminating bad elements is a form of development because these negative forces hinder progress. Therefore, if cosmic powers are destroying or eliminating harmful people or energies, it is still the utilization of power for growth. On Earth, there have been frequent misuses of power. When Queen Kaikeyi forced King Dashrath to exile Lord Ram, it was a misuse of power. When Bali forced Sugreev to leave the kingdom and kept his wife, it was the misuse of power. When Ravana abducted Goddess Sita, it was the misuse of power. When Duryodhana and Dushasana insulted Draupadi in the assembly, it was the misuse of power. Interestingly, all of these individuals were well aware that they would face the consequences of their actions, yet they became blinded by their own power. The powerful often believe that no one can defeat them, but they forget that the most powerful force is the universe and the cosmic powers. These forces will not leave you. Today, everyone—from a policeman to a king—is misusing power. We forget to learn from our history that this soil is the graveyard of many advanced civilizations. They made great progress in terms of material development but failed to adopt spiritual growth, which ultimately led to their demise.

Our new generation should focus on the development of spiritual strength. This does not mean mere worship or wearing specific clothes. It means being kind-hearted, honest, and always standing for what is right.

****

CHAPTER - 22

Long-Term Rule

Throughout history, the endurance of empires and rulers has hinged not merely on military might but on their ability to integrate with and respect the societies they governed. The Mughal Empire, reigning from 1528 to 1750, boasted one of the largest armies globally, with estimates suggesting a strength ranging from 911,400 to over 4 million infantry and 342,696 cavalry during the 17th century.

Despite this formidable force, the Mughals were eventually supplanted by the British, another foreign power, who, though militarily advanced, faced expulsion by a relatively small, unarmed Congress movement. This sequence of events underscores that the longevity of rule is influenced by factors beyond sheer strength.

The Mughals' inability to fully assimilate into Indian society led many locals to favour the British, perceiving them as a preferable alternative. However, the British, despite their advancements, erred by disrespecting and exploiting Indians, siphoning wealth to Britain—a sentiment epitomized by the transfer of treasures like the Kohinoor diamond. This blatant disregard for the native populace sowed seeds of discontent, culminating in their eventual ousting.

India's susceptibility to foreign domination can also be traced to internal societal divisions. The rigid caste system marginalized lower castes, subjecting them to oppressive conditions. Consequently, when the Mughals invaded, these oppressed groups often viewed the foreign rulers as liberators compared to their indigenous oppressors.

In contrast, the ideal ruler is exemplified by figures like Lord Rama, whose reign in Ayodhya is celebrated for justice, compassion, and unwavering commitment to the welfare of all subjects, irrespective of their status. Such leadership fosters unity and resilience against external threats.

In contemporary times, echoes of past mistakes persist. A widening chasm between the affluent and the impoverished, coupled with governance that mirrors the detachment of erstwhile foreign rulers, risks alienating the populace. Neglecting the needs of the underprivileged and perpetuating systemic inequities can pave the way for instability and external exploitation.

Sustainable and enduring governance necessitates empathy, inclusivity, and equitable development. Leaders must embody the virtues of historical paragons like Lord Rama, prioritizing the well-being of all citizens to cultivate a harmonious and resilient society.

****

CHAPTER - 23

The Failure of Azad Hind Fauj

The Azad Hind Fauj, or the Indian National Army (INA), was established during World War II with the aim of securing India's independence from British rule. Led by Subhas Chandra Bose, the INA allied with the Axis powers, notably Japan and Nazi Germany, to challenge British authority in India. However, this alliance and the subsequent military campaigns faced significant challenges, leading to the eventual failure of the INA's objectives.

One of the critical miscalculations was the decision to collaborate with Axis powers, particularly Japan. While Japan provided military support and resources, their primary interest lay in expanding their own empire rather than genuinely supporting Indian independence. This alliance led to the perception of the INA as a puppet state, undermining its legitimacy among Indians and the international community.

The INA participated in key battles such as the Battle of Imphal, aiming to penetrate British defenses in India. However, these campaigns were met with fierce resistance from the British Indian Army, leading to significant casualties and retreats. The lack of adequate training, resources, and support from local populations further hampered the INA's effectiveness.

The INA's military actions, in conjunction with Japanese forces, had unintended humanitarian consequences. The disruption of supply chains and agricultural production contributed to the Bengal Famine of 1943, resulting in the loss of millions of lives. This tragedy highlighted the devastating impact of war strategies that failed to consider the well-being of civilian populations.

The failure of the Azad Hind Fauj underscores the complexities of aligning with foreign powers whose interests may not align with national aspirations. It also emphasizes the importance of strategic planning that prioritizes both military objectives and the welfare of the civilian population. Understanding these historical lessons is crucial for future movements seeking to balance the pursuit of political goals with ethical considerations.

****

CHAPTER - 24

Artificial Intelligence

The human body is an extraordinary creation, equipped with a natural system of intelligence that is unparalleled in its complexity and capability. At the core of this system is the mind, which functions as the processor, orchestrating thoughts, emotions, and actions in a seamless manner. This natural intelligence is not merely a byproduct of evolution; it is a profound gift that enables us to navigate the world, make decisions, and create meaning in our lives.

The Mind as the Ultimate Processor

The human mind is often compared to a computer, with the brain serving as its hardware and thoughts as its software. However, this comparison, while useful in some contexts, falls short of capturing the true essence of the mind's capabilities. Unlike any man-made machine, the mind processes information in a way that is deeply integrated with our emotions, consciousness, and sense of self. It has the ability to learn, adapt, and grow continuously, driven by both external stimuli and internal reflections.

The mind's processing power is not limited to logical reasoning or data analysis. It also encompasses creativity, empathy, intuition, and the ability to understand abstract concepts such as love, beauty, and morality. These are areas where artificial intelligence, despite its impressive advancements, struggles to replicate the depth and nuance of human thought.

The Rise of Artificial Intelligence

In recent years, artificial intelligence (AI) has emerged as a powerful tool, designed to augment and, in some cases, replicate human cognitive functions. AI systems can perform tasks such as data processing, pattern recognition, and decision-making at speeds and scales that far surpass human capabilities. These systems have revolutionized industries, from healthcare and finance to entertainment and transportation.

However, it is crucial to recognize the fundamental differences between AI and the natural intelligence inherent in the human mind. AI, by its very nature, is artificial. It operates based on algorithms, which are sets of rules created by humans to solve specific problems. While AI can simulate certain aspects of human thought, it lacks the consciousness, emotional depth, and ethical reasoning that define true intelligence.

The Incomparable Gift of Natural Intelligence

The term "artificial" itself highlights the limitations of AI when compared to the natural intelligence bestowed upon us. While AI can process vast amounts of data and perform complex calculations, it does so without awareness or understanding. It cannot experience emotions, appreciate art, or engage in moral reasoning. These are the domains where human intelligence excels, offering a richness and depth that machines simply cannot replicate.

God, or the forces of nature, depending on one's beliefs, has endowed humanity with a unique gift—the ability to think, feel, and create in ways that are profoundly interconnected with the fabric of existence. This natural intelligence allows us to experience life in its full spectrum, from the joy of a sunset to the sorrow of loss, from the thrill of discovery to the peace of meditation.

Cultivating the Mind's Full Potential

In an age where technology is advancing rapidly, it is easy to become overly reliant on artificial tools, sometimes at the expense of our natural abilities. While AI can undoubtedly assist us in various aspects of life, it is important not to let these tools overshadow our inherent intelligence. Instead, we should strive to cultivate and enhance our natural cognitive and emotional capabilities.

One of the most effective ways to do this is through continuous learning and self-reflection. Engaging with challenging ideas, reading books that expand our horizons, and practicing mindfulness are all ways to sharpen the mind and deepen our understanding of the world. Additionally, cultivating emotional intelligence—our ability to recognize, understand, and manage our own emotions and those of others—is equally important in achieving personal and collective well-being.

The practice of meditation, for example, has been shown to improve focus, reduce stress, and enhance emotional regulation. Similarly, engaging in creative activities such as writing, painting, or music can stimulate different areas of the brain, fostering innovation and deeper emotional expression.

The Role of Ethics in Intelligence

Another key aspect of natural intelligence is its ethical dimension. Unlike AI, which follows programmed instructions, human intelligence operates within a framework of values and morals. This ethical reasoning is what allows us to make decisions that consider the well-being of others, to act with compassion, and to strive for justice.

In a world increasingly influenced by AI, it is essential that we do not lose sight of these ethical considerations. While AI can assist in making decisions, it is up to us, as humans, to ensure that these decisions are made with wisdom and integrity. This requires a strong ethical foundation, something that can only be developed through conscious effort and reflection.

Conclusion: Embracing Our Natural Intelligence

The creation of artificial intelligence is a testament to the ingenuity and creativity of the human mind. However, it is crucial to remember that AI, no matter how advanced, remains a tool—a reflection of our own intelligence rather than a replacement for it. As we continue to develop and integrate AI into our lives, we must also invest in cultivating our natural intelligence, ensuring that our minds remain sharp, our hearts compassionate, and our spirits wise.

By embracing our natural intelligence and nurturing it through education, ethical living, and creative expression, we can unlock the full potential of our minds and live more fulfilling, meaningful lives. The future of humanity lies not in the machines we create, but in the wisdom and understanding that only we, as sentient beings, can achieve.

****

CHAPTER - 25

Ancient Wisdom

My father was smelling monsoon by seeing ant moving in big line with food means they started storing food during rain so there is rain expected soon. My grandfather, a farmer was feeling snake nearby listing increasing chirping of sparrow, I learned from my grandmother was knowing too much effective remedies from local natural things. My mother was smelling monsoon near seeing a crow building nest.

They were living a healthy and long life without any artificial support, whereas after development of over 67000 medicines for around 800 type disease, we are neither in position to remove the diseases nor keeping us healthy besides the fact that our life becoming shorter.

The reason behind it is we are going far from nature. We are dependent on artificial facilities, the mixtures of profits and poor quality products, material and thoughts.

So, we need to understand our earth, our nature, our cosmic systems, our universe and various things made by god not by man. The effect of purity, the effect of energy, the meaning and purpose of sunlight, the power of gravity, and the system through which moon affects our sea causing high tide. The water which is remain with us in same quantity after billions of year, the air which is remain with us, the never ending sunlight, the soil with power of fertility, the tree providing food, fruits from nature proves that there is power surrounding us taking care of our lives.

Life is too much precious so we need to keep it safe, long and healthy. Our each diet is important, each breath is important, each night is important, peace of every second is important. How we can do it. Of course we have to go close to nature universe and god rather mall movie and race for money.

When god has given everything without any cost, when god is taking care of ourselves round the clock, we also need to take care of those who are less fortunate and struggling for food and health issues. How we can be a educated when we cant understand it. We cant understand the message of god. May be we are advanced in modern science but far behind from old spiritual science which much more advanced and was connected to cosmic science.

****

CHAPTER - 26

Cosmic Interference

Our actions—past, present, and future aspirations—are often influenced by cosmic forces. Occasionally, we experience spontaneous thoughts or ideas that seem to emerge from beyond our usual patterns of thinking. At times, an inner strength propels us toward actions that align with our best interests, while at other moments, an internal voice cautions us against certain decisions. These intuitive signals can be positive, negative, or neutral, guiding us in various ways.

This phenomenon aligns with the concept of karma, where our deeds—good, bad, or accumulated over time—yield corresponding outcomes. Notably, extraordinary actions can lead to specific, sometimes unforeseen, results. This suggests the presence of an omnipresent intelligence meticulously assessing our behaviors and their consequences, interacting with us on a spiritual level through our minds and hearts.

Such notions are echoed in ancient philosophical texts. For instance, Yagnakaya, a revered sage from the Brihadaranyaka Upanishad, delved into the nature of the self and consciousness. He proposed that dreams are active projections of the self, indicating that our imaginative experiences share the creative essence of ultimate reality. This perspective underscores the profound connection between individual consciousness and the broader cosmos.

Therefore, it is plausible to consider that a higher intelligence or universal system monitors and responds to our actions and intentions. This system, existing as energy and waves, envelops us continually. We are under constant observation, not merely by earthly entities but by this universal intelligence. Consequently, it is imperative to remain mindful of our actions and deeds, recognizing that they are perpetually under the scrutiny of this cosmic system.

****

CHAPTER - 27

The Artificial Life

In this digital world, the line between what is real and what is fake is becoming increasingly blurred. People are drawn into the allure of instant gratification—fame, success, or even a momentary sense of superiority—all created through artificial means. The artificial life is one where people live for the approval of others, showcasing a version of themselves that may not align with their inner values. It is a life that thrives on appearances and neglects the importance of honesty and authenticity.

India, with its rich cultural heritage and spiritual depth, must resist falling prey to this trend of superficial living. It is time for the nation to step out of the shadow of this "photos hopped" existence and embrace the values that have long defined its greatness. The best practices—ethics, righteousness, integrity—should not merely be performed for the sake of appearances. They should flow from the heart, be embedded in our culture, and become second nature to each individual.

True culture is not something that can be fabricated or showcased for approval. It is something that lives and breathes within us. A truly cultured individual or society does not need to create a false picture to impress others. Instead, they live by the principles of kindness, honesty, and morality, not just as an act but as an inherent part of their being. India's history is filled with examples of individuals who lived by these values, not for public applause but because they believed in the rightness of their actions.

The rise of social media has given us tools to connect with the world, but it has also fueled the desire to present a perfect life—a life that may not be real. The real challenge for individuals and businesses in this new era is to move beyond this urge to create an illusion. India must return to its roots and embrace the values that bring authentic happiness and true success.

Ultimately, no matter how sophisticated our tools become, or how well we can manipulate images and perceptions, true character and integrity will always stand out. People will remember us not for the pictures we post or the stories we fabricate but for the genuineness of our actions and the purity of our hearts. India's path to greatness lies not in its ability to project an image but in its ability to live by values that inspire trust, respect, and love.

Living authentically, with integrity and purpose, is the only way to break free from the trap of superficiality. Only when we focus on building character over reputation, and ethics over appearances, can we truly build a society that is strong, resilient, and worthy of admiration.

Let us remember: the soul is the only witness that matters. Let us live lives that reflect our highest potential, not as a reflection of what we want others to see, but as a true expression of who we are.

****

CHAPTER - 28

Life Is The Toughest Examination

In every examination, time management is the most critical factor. You have to solve questions within a limited period. The same applies to life; the examination of life also comes with a fixed time limit. While people often think that human life spans an average of 100 years, in reality, the effective working period is only about 45 years.

Every day consists of 24 hours, but we spend 8 hours sleeping, 30 minutes on daily routines, and at least 1.5 hours on meals and snacks, totaling 10 hours dedicated to essential activities for sustaining life. This leaves us with 14 hours a day. Over a 100-year lifespan, this adds up to 57 working years. However, if we subtract childhood (approximately 12 years), we are left with just 45 years of active work. Further subtracting time spent on illnesses, travel, and the necessary work to earn a livelihood, the actual time available for life's real purpose is even shorter.

The true examination of life lies in how w e conduct ourselves:

- How do we behave with our family and society?
- Do we earn our livelihood ethically or unethically?
- Are we humble, kind, and honest?
- Do we help the poor and vulnerable?
- How much time do we dedicate to worship, understanding the universe, and leading a purposeful life?

Our current life should be meaningful and exemplary, ensuring that we are deserving of a better, more fulfilling existence in the future—a life that may span thousands of years. Conversely, wasting time on gossip, fighting, jealousy, or enmity detracts from the real purpose of life and is a squandered opportunity.

Regardless of age—young or old—people should reflect on how much time they have left to secure their "seat" in a better life. Returning to this world in the same form is akin to repeating a grade in school, a sign of failure to fulfil life's purpose.

Life has a clear purpose. Do not waste it.

****

CHAPTER - 29

Method To Reach God - Physical And Spiritual

Humanity's quest to connect with the divine has been pursued through two primary avenues: the spiritual path, deeply rooted in ancient traditions, and the physical path, exemplified by modern scientific endeavours such as space exploration.

Spiritual connectivity involves reaching the divine through inner practices like meditation and contemplation. Historically, sages and mystics dedicated years to meditation in seclusion, seeking purity and enlightenment. This path requires profound dedication and inner purity, qualities that are often challenging to cultivate amidst the distractions of contemporary society. Today, many attempt to connect with the divine through brief rituals or prayers, but true spiritual connectivity demands a deeper commitment.

On the physical front, humanity has made remarkable strides in exploring the cosmos. Technological advancements have enabled us to send spacecraft to distant planets, expanding our understanding of the universe. For instance, NASA's recent launch of the Sphere X observatory aims to create a 3D map of over 100 million stars in the Milky Way and 450 million galaxies beyond, seeking answers to fundamental questions about the universe and the potential for life beyond Earth.

Looking ahead, the proposed Habitable Worlds Observatory (HWO) is designed to directly image and analyze Earth-sized exoplanets in the habitable zones of their stars. Scheduled for launch in the 2040s, HWO aims to identify and study potentially habitable worlds, searching for chemical biosignatures in their atmospheres, such as oxygen and methane, which could indicate the presence of life.

As we stand at this crossroads, humanity has the opportunity to pursue both spiritual and physical paths to connect with the divine and explore new realms. The spiritual path calls for inner transformation and dedication, while the physical path leverages technological advancements to reach beyond our planet. Both paths require commitment, purity of intention, and a vision that transcends personal gain, aiming for the betterment of all beings.

The choices we make today will shape the future of our civilization. Embracing both spiritual wisdom and scientific exploration can lead us to profound discoveries, enriching our understanding of the universe and our place within it.

****

CHAPTER - 30

Live Like Brothers Or Enemies

The worst invention done by human civilization was Dynamite and now it is Nuclear Bomb which can remove whole human civilization. Now it is important for humans is to find counter of dynamite and nuclear. If if some one has used the nuclear weapon there should be counter of it. Like we develop cure of every virus we need to find the cure of damaging weapons. The counter attack increased the damages. This is not the solution. In fact humans are developing counter more powerful weapons instead of cure. This universe has solution of very problem and whole universal power exist in our mind, so it is not difficult to find solution of any problem. This is question of survivarl of human civilization.

The history shows that many great human civilization had been vanished like Mahamaya, Sumerian, Babylonia , Anunnaki , Egyptian, Aryan etc. No one know the exact reason. All is only imagination of causes but the thing which is certain is that if we will not defuse all bombs or will not find counter of damages, there will always be possibility that human civilization is vanished in few days.

This is most important topic we all must understand and should work for most urgent innovations. A Cure for Destructive Weapons. These weapons are capable of obliterating entire cities and wiping out human civilization. As a society that has thrived on innovation, humans have reached a point where technological advancements are no longer just tools for progress but also pose the greatest threat to our very existence. The urgent need of our time is to discover a countermeasure, not only to the use of nuclear weapons but to the destructive potential of all such devices.

Alfred Nobel, the inventor of dynamite, once said, "My dynamite will sooner lead to peace than a thousand world conventions. As soon as men will find that in one instant, whole armies can be utterly destroyed, they surely will abide by golden peace." Ironically, this belief was misplaced. Instead of leading to peace, it paved the way for more powerful and destructive weapons like nuclear bombs, capable of erasing human civilizations in seconds.

The fundamental flaw in this thinking is that counterattacks and the development of stronger weapons in response to threats have become a vicious cycle. The competition to outdo one another with more advanced weaponry only escalates the dangers, rather than offering security or solutions. History shows that the arms race does not lead to peace; it leads to greater destruction.

The real innovation that humankind must focus on today is not more powerful weapons, but a way to neutralize the damage caused by existing ones. Much like how scientists work tirelessly to find cures for viruses, there must be a concerted effort to discover remedies or neutralizing technologies for destructive forces like nuclear weapons. As Mahatma Gandhi once said, "An eye for an eye will make the whole world blind." A world where nations continue to develop increasingly powerful weapons will eventually reach a point where destruction outpaces any hope of recovery.

Instead of furthering this cycle of destruction, humanity should channel its intellectual and technological resources into finding ways to prevent the devastation of such weapons—before they are ever used.

The universe, with all its mysteries and natural laws, contains solutions to every problem—if only we seek them. The human mind is one of the most powerful forces in the universe, capable of creating and destroying in equal measure. As Albert Einstein famously said, "We cannot solve our problems with the same thinking we used when we created them." It is time for humanity to rise above the narrow mindset of destruction and instead seek solutions that preserve life and civilization.

The mind that invented the nuclear bomb is the same mind that can discover how to counter it. The challenge lies in harnessing this potential not for warfare but for protection, sustainability, and survival.

History has shown us the fragility of human existence. Great civilizations like the Maya, Sumerians, Babylonians, Egyptians, and Aryans have all vanished, and while the reasons remain unclear, there is a common theme: civilizations collapse when they fail to solve their greatest challenges. Whether through internal decay, environmental disaster, or warfare, their downfall serves as a reminder that survival is never guaranteed. The modern world, too, faces the possibility of extinction—not through natural means but by our own hands.

The question is no longer just about how we thrive, but how we avoid a catastrophe of our own making. If we do not defuse the ticking time bombs of today—nuclear, biological, and chemical weapons—we may follow in the footsteps of these lost civilizations. And unlike past societies, which faded over centuries, we risk vanishing in a matter of days or even hours.

The innovation humanity must pursue now is a global effort to neutralize destructive forces, whether through technological advancements, diplomatic agreements, or international cooperation. As Martin Luther King Jr. said, "We must learn to live together as brothers or perish together as fools." The path to survival lies in unity, wisdom, and innovation aimed at preserving life, not taking it.

It is time for us to refocus our creative and intellectual energies towards finding solutions to the problems we have created. As we stand at this critical juncture in history, the future of our civilization depends on our ability to innovate for peace and survival. The survival of human civilization itself hangs in the balance, and the most pressing challenge we face is the urgent need to innovate our way to a safer, more sustainable world.

****

CHAPTER - 31

War Against Hunger And Injustice

The human civilization has to start a war against hunger and injustice. This is missing from every country, every state and every mind. Justice and Food should be within the reach of everyone. The human civilization has to fight against hunger and injustice. This is the biggest worship of god. This issue transcend borders, cultures, and generations, demanding our collective action and unwavering commitment.

Hunger remains a pervasive problem worldwide. According to recent reports, progress against global hunger has largely stagnated since 2015, with crises multiplying and intensifying, leading to severe hunger affecting more people.

The 2023 Global Hunger Index highlights that, after years of advancement up to 2015, progress against hunger worldwide remains largely at a standstill. As the effects of crises multiply and intensify, more and more people are experiencing severe hunger, with the situation expected to worsen throughout the year. Large demographic groups, such as women and youth, are bearing the brunt of these crises.

The civilization need to have a sustainable Agricultural Practices for long term growth of agriculture production. Investing in agricultural research and embracing new technologies, such as genetically modified crops and artificial intelligence, can boost food production sustainably.

An open letter by the World Food Prize Foundation, supported by renowned scientists, calls for a "moonshot" in agricultural research to prevent a food crisis expected by 2050.

In India the congress government had started the Mid Day Meal policy where all students were getting food. This is a great still working and giving food to poor children who are getting education and food both. The equitable Food Distribution ensuring that food reaches those in need involves improving infrastructure, reducing waste, and addressing market inefficiencies.

The another major issue is in fact the justice is not in reach of poor. The system of corruption in courts, advocate don't charge fees , they try to extort money based on financial capability of client and case. The more people are fighting to save criminal than sufferer. Streamlining legal processes and ensuring timely justice are crucial. Injustice manifests in various forms, from systemic discrimination to unequal access to opportunities.

In India, there should be necessary to record court proceedings and upload it on portal so that performance of advocate, knowledge of advocate could be assessed by higher court. The judgements are written without reading the papers that's why most of the time it is incorrect. For incorrect judgement, there should be punishment to judge also. Moreover, the expenses of providing justice should be within the scope of government. Now days, a person do not have money cannot get justice. Government officials like police is filing false cases to extort money and government fight the wrong case. All this is harassment of poor public by government itself.

A Call to Action

Eradicating hunger and injustice is not merely an act of charity but a moral imperative. It requires:

Collective Responsibility: Governments, organizations, and individuals must collaborate, recognizing that the well-being of one impacts all.

Sustained Commitment: Long-term strategies, rather than short-term fixes, are essential for meaningful change.

Empathy and Compassion: Understanding and addressing the needs of the marginalized strengthen the fabric of our societies.

In conclusion, the fight against hunger and injustice is the greatest service we can render to humanity. Let us unite in this endeavor, ensuring that every individual has access to food and justice, thereby honouring the intrinsic dignity of all.

****

CHAPTER - 32

Shift Of Power

The shift of power from common citizens to a select few has redirected India's focus from "development of the country" to "development of companies." This centralization of power threatens India's vitality unless authority is returned to the populace. The Micro, Small, and Medium Enterprises (MSME) sector, which provides employment to over 110 million individuals, is struggling despite financial assistance. This struggle is exacerbated by the concentration of wealth among the rich, leading to a decline in the purchasing power of the general population. Consequently, the end-user's purchasing power has shrunk, limiting consumption to a wealthy minority. This imbalance hampers economic growth and undermines the foundational strength of the MSME sector. India will die if the power will not be re-shift to common people of India.

The development of country counts from the increasing

The financial development brings happiness and mental growth. The poor first focus on earning money for food whereas the sound financial position turns a person to contribute on spiritual growth and development and gives space to go for innovations. The barrier of need of food stops all innovative goals and development. Hence, a country has to make their people financial rich so that the everybody starts contributing over mental and innovative development. The transfer of power and wealth from common person to only few rich kills the country. India cannot develop only take a dip in Ganga, India can be developed only through financial and education development.

The happiness comes from financial and educational enrichment rather taking a dip in Ganga.

You can expect peace without justice. The equality of wealth and happiness among all. The kings and kingdom are only self centred development, whereas the democracy gives happiness to all but democracy cannot be expected from few rich participating in election and running the country like kings.

Indian civilization has witnessed a long SLAVE STATUS because of hits habit of transfer power and health from common citizen to few rich. The inequality, injustice and power divide the people.

****

CHAPTER - 33

No Religion Land

The prevalence of unethical behaviours such as greed, hatred, dowry, and bribery in society indicates a significant shortfall in character development within our education system. Despite formal education, individuals, including those in esteemed positions like government officials and law enforcement, often engage in corrupt practices, suggesting that education alone has not effectively instilled ethical values.

This scenario reflects a societal focus on material wealth, often pursued through unethical means, leading to a deviation from 'Dharma'—the moral and righteous path as outlined in sacred texts like the Vedas, Ramayana, and Bhagavad Gita. Dharma encompasses duties, rights, laws, conduct, virtues, and the 'right way of living' . However, when these principles are not adhered to, society becomes devoid of true righteousness, engaging in superficial religious practices without embodying the core ethical teachings.

Historical narratives illustrate that divine figures such as Lord Rama and Lord Krishna aligned themselves with righteousness, supporting individuals who upheld Dharma. These stories serve as moral guides, yet contemporary society often engages with them superficially, neglecting to internalize and practice their teachings.

The universe operates on principles of order and obedience, with celestial bodies following precise paths, exemplifying harmony and adherence to natural laws. In contrast, human society frequently exhibits disobedience and ethical breaches, leading to societal decay.

To avert potential self-destruction, it is imperative to realign our lives with ethical principles, fostering a society that values character and righteousness over material gain.

****

CHAPTER - 34

The Big Giant On Earth

In Rig Veda, it is mentioned that before human shifted from 7 star (Sapt Rishi Mandal) the big gains were ruling on earth. The modern science confirms the presence of Dinosaurs scientifically. The Dragan are very much worshiped in China. The Indian temples situated at southern region of India showing the architecture of big giants in every temple. These big giants were friendly to human. It is unfortunate the India could not preserve the detail of these big giants who were friendly to human. They were living in sea that's why all the temple situated near those cities which are located near sea there structures are given. While meeting with various old peoples in Chennai, Madurai etc cities, they confirmed that these giants were very familiar with humans. They were protecting to humans.

The China and India are neighbours. Both the countries have sea sours. The China was very much protected by Dragons. The Dragons are symbol or prosperity so it is very much confirm that the Dragons were friendly to human.

DRAGONS - THE GIANT SNAKE IN CHINIESE MYTHOLOGY

Dragons in Chinese Mythology: The Giant Snake-Like Creatures Dragons hold a prominent place in Chinese mythology, symbolizing power, strength, prosperity, and auspiciousness. Unlike the fearsome and destructive depictions of dragons in Western mythology, Chinese dragons are often portrayed as benevolent creatures. They are more snake-like in their appearance and are associated with water, weather, and the cosmos.

The Origin of Dragons in Chinese Mythology: Dragons in Chinese culture trace back thousands of years, to early depictions on pottery and artifacts, representing the harmonious blending of various creatures, particularly snakes. Over time, dragons evolved in both appearance and symbolism, becoming legendary creatures that played a central role in myths and folklore.

The Chinese dragon is not a singular figure but a composite of many creatures:

Serpentine body: The dragon's long, snake-like body represents flexibility, grace, and fluid movement. This ties them to the rivers, seas, and rainfall.

Claws of an eagle: Symbolizing power.

Horns of a deer: Representing nobility and strength.

Scales of a fish: Connecting them to water and oceans.

Dragons in China are believed to embody the ideal traits of all these animals, forming a creature that is both wise and powerful.

In their earliest depictions, Chinese dragons were often represented as snake-like, reflecting the Chinese reverence for the serpent. In many ancient cultures, including China, snakes were seen as symbols of rebirth, immortality, and transformation due to their ability to shed their skin. As dragons evolved into mythical creatures, this serpentine form persisted, making them appear like giant, divine snakes.

In Chinese mythology, dragons are often depicted as large, elongated beings that are agile and graceful, despite their immense size. They have the ability to fly without wings and are known for controlling natural forces, particularly rain and rivers. While Western dragons are associated with fire, Chinese dragons are creatures of water.

Dragons as Symbols of Power and Weather : Chinese dragons are closely connected to the natural elements, particularly water, and are often viewed as controllers of the weather, especially rain. They are seen as bringers of rain, essential for agriculture, and thus symbolizing life and prosperity.

Rain-Bringers: Dragons are believed to control rivers, seas, and rains. When ancient Chinese people prayed for rain, they prayed to dragons.

Many ancient rituals and festivals were conducted in honour of dragons to seek their favour and ensure good weather for crops.

River Dragons: In some legends, specific rivers are governed by dragons, which are believed to live in underwater palaces. These river dragons are said to watch over waterways and protect their flow, ensuring the prosperity of the lands they nourish. Many ancient Chinese myths involve dragons playing key roles in the creation of the universe and the fate of humanity:

The Dragon King: The Dragon King, also called the Long Wang, is the ruler of the seas and rivers. There are four Dragon Kings, each ruling over one of the seas surrounding China: the East Sea, South Sea, West Sea, and North Sea. They were responsible for sending rain to the land and protecting the people.

In many stories, the Dragon King interacts with emperors or gods to ensure a balance in nature. He is often asked to bring rain during times of drought or withhold it when floods threaten.

Nüwa and the Great Flood: In one version of the myth about Nüwa, the creator goddess, a great flood threatens to destroy the earth. Nüwa uses the body of a dragon to patch the hole in the sky and stop the flood. This tale emphasizes the connection between dragons, water, and life-saving power.

The Yellow Emperor (Huangdi) and the Dragon: One of the most famous legends involving dragons is that of the Yellow Emperor. According to legend, after ruling over China and uniting the people, the Yellow Emperor transformed into a dragon and ascended to the heavens, symbolizing the connection between dragons and emperors as divine rulers.

Dragons in Modern Chinese Culture

Dragons continue to play a vital role in Chinese festivals, literature, art, and cinema. They are still seen as powerful symbols of good fortune, strength, and wisdom. The Chinese people regard themselves as descendants of the dragon, a claim stemming from the belief that the early emperors were born from the dragons.

In Chinese mythology, dragons are much more than mythical creatures; they are ancient, snake-like beings that embody the very forces of nature and the universe. They are revered as protectors, weather controllers, and symbols of power, prosperity, and wisdom. The mythology surrounding them reflects their central place in Chinese culture, serving as a reminder of the interconnectedness between humanity, nature, and the divine.

Since the Vedas hare having very true picture and history of hearth, the information given in Rig Veda about big giants (Refer my book- Ved – Decoding the Mystery of Universe) should be taken as matter of research. We should understand this the universe never destroy its own creation. All such creatures have been shifted to another planet. The shifting is very easy just for few second shift the gravity and the whole sea or earth can be shifted anywhere.

The detail about these big giants can be a available in old manuscripts of different countries. We need to do research so that can trace their whereabouts and a great friendships of human and big giants which can open a great door of development.

****

CHAPTER - 35

Who Made The Soul

The one of the biggest question exist in society that whether god exist or not. Whether someone is watching us or not. Who is running the universe. Is that power is God or the existence of universe is a combination of material and chemicals.

The answer lives in another question and that is WHO MADE SOULD. Our science know many things, secretes of universe, physics, chemistry, mathematics, the construction of body, how to repair it but one thing we don't know WHOE MADE SOUL. Why our body dies. What is the system which generates power in body. How the consciousness works.

The soul is definitely made by god and that is the proof that god exist. The soul is energy. It has no shape, it has consciousness, it talks, it suggests, its differentiate between good and bad. It alerts us.

So the god exist. God is everywhere in form of energy. We are because the god is. We mean our soul. Without soul se are just dust. So if we the human civilization will understand that god exist and our purpose of life is to reach to that level then there will be no war, there will be no enmity among people.

The soul never die so we are immortal. Our body will die but not the soul. The most important research is to know about soul means to know about God. The soul, often described as energy, lacks a tangible form but possesses consciousness, the ability to communicate, discern between good and bad, and provide guidance. It is in the essence of the soul that the presence of God finds affirmation. This energy, intangible and yet deeply influential, serves as evidence of a higher power.

God, in this perspective, permeates every facet of existence in the form of energy. Recognizing this divine presence could potentially unite humanity in a shared understanding of purpose. If we acknowledge the existence of God and comprehend our life's purpose as aspiring to reach a higher spiritual level, the potential for conflict and animosity diminishes. Crucially, the assertion that the soul is immortal reinforces the idea that our existence extends beyond the temporal confines of our physical bodies. While our bodies may succumb to mortality, the eternal nature of the soul underscores our inherent immortality.

In light of these reflections, a profound avenue of research emerges – the exploration of the soul. Understanding the soul becomes synonymous with comprehending the nature of God. If human civilization collectively embraces this pursuit, envisioning a purposeful existence aligned with spiritual growth, the prospect of wars and enmity among people may significantly diminish. In essence, unravelling the mysteries of the soul becomes the gateway to understanding the divine and embracing a more harmonious coexistence.

****

CHAPTER - 36

On The Pages Of History

History is not merely a record of past events; it is the very fabric that weaves together the narratives of human existence. From the rise and fall of empires to the whispers of everyday lives, history holds the stories of those who dared to dream, to challenge the status quo, and to leave their indelible marks on the world. In this context, the notion of becoming a legend is not just an aspiration; it is a call to action. To be immortal on the pages of history is to embody the virtues of courage, resilience, and vision that transcend time.

Legends are forged in the crucible of extraordinary circumstances. They are not merely born from accolades or titles, but from the spirit of perseverance and the willingness to fight for one's beliefs. Figures such as Mahatma Gandhi, Nelson Mandela, and Marie Curie have become timeless icons not solely for their accomplishments but for their unwavering commitment to justice, equality, and knowledge. Their stories resonate through time, teaching us that true greatness is often rooted in humility and the pursuit of a greater good.

Courage in the Face of Adversity; History is replete with tales of individuals who stood firm in the face of overwhelming odds. The courage displayed by Joan of Arc, who led her people against the English forces despite her youth and gender, illustrates how the audacity to act can change the course of history. The legend of Joan teaches us that the heart of a warrior does not shy away from challenges; instead, it embraces them, igniting the flames of hope in others.

Resilience in Pursuit of Dreams: The journey of history is often fraught with setbacks and failures. Yet, it is the resilience to rise after each fall that paves the way for greatness. Thomas Edison, whose tireless experiments eventually led to the invention of the electric light bulb, famously stated, "I have not failed. I've just found 10,000 ways that won't work." Such unwavering determination is the hallmark of legends, reminding us that each setback is merely a stepping stone toward success.

Vision Beyond the Horizon: Legends are visionaries who see possibilities where others see obstacles. Albert Einstein, with his revolutionary theories, redefined our understanding of the universe. His quote, "Imagination is more important than knowledge," encapsulates the essence of being a legend. To immortalize oneself in history, one must dare to envision a future that transcends current limitations, inspiring generations to come.

Crafting Your Legacy: While the past may be filled with remarkable stories, the present is an opportunity to pen your own. Each individual has the potential to contribute to history through their actions, beliefs, and choices. To be a legend is to live with purpose, to strive for excellence, and to leave a positive impact on the world around you. Here are ways to start crafting your legacy:

Embrace Your Unique Path: Understand that your journey is uniquely yours. Celebrate your individuality and the contributions you can make to your community, society, or even the world.

Stand for What You Believe: Advocate for causes that resonate with you. Whether through activism, philanthropy, or simply raising awareness, your voice can echo through time.

Cultivate Compassion and Empathy: Legends are remembered for their kindness as much as their achievements. Strive to make a difference in the lives of others, fostering a legacy of love and compassion.

Pursue Knowledge and Growth: Commit to lifelong learning and self-improvement. The pursuit of knowledge not only enriches your life but also enables you to inspire and educate others.

History is a living testament to the power of the human spirit. It reminds us that our actions, however small, can ripple through time, influencing the lives of those who come after us. To become a legend is not a pursuit for the faint-hearted; it requires passion, perseverance, and an unwavering commitment to leaving the world a better place than you found it. So, seize the moment, embrace your potential, and strive to be immortal on the pages of history. In doing so, you will not only become a legend but also inspire others to follow in your footsteps, ensuring that the story of humanity continues to thrive.

****

CHAPTER - 37

Kumari Kandam

Kumari Kandam is a mythical lost continent believed by some to have existed south of present-day India, in the Indian Ocean. According to Tamil legends, this submerged landmass was once home to an advanced Tamil civilization. The concept of Kumari Kandam has been linked to the 19th-century hypothesis of Lemuria—a proposed lost continent intended to explain geological and biological similarities between Africa, India, and Madagascar. While the Lemuria theory has been discredited by modern plate tectonics, the idea of Kumari Kandam remains significant in Tamil cultural narratives.

The term "Kumari Kandam" first appeared in the 15th-century Tamil text Kanda Puranam, a version of the Skanda Purana. In this text, the Earth is divided into several continents, one of which is ruled by a maiden named Kumari, giving rise to the name "Kumari Kandam" ("Kumari's Continent"). In the early 20th century, Tamil revivalists adopted this term to describe the purported lost Tamil continent, integrating it into their cultural and historical narratives.

The myth of Kumari Kandam holds substantial cultural importance, particularly among Tamil nationalists and revivalists. It is often portrayed as the cradle of Tamil civilization, symbolizing the antiquity and richness of Tamil culture and language. This narrative has been utilized to assert the historical significance of the Tamil people and to promote a sense of pride and identity.

From a scientific standpoint, there is no evidence to support the existence of Kumari Kandam as a lost continent. The concept of continental drift and the understanding of plate tectonics have provided explanations for the current distribution of continents without invoking lost landmasses like Lemuria or Kumari Kandam. Therefore, while the idea remains a fascinating aspect of regional mythology, it is not recognized in contemporary geology.

The science try to get facts whereas there cannot be any proof of those things which has vanished and mixed up with elements of universe. I do not have any proof about my grandfather. No one has saw the earth more than 120 years of his life, it does not mean there was nothing before that. In fact the history, the books, the religion concepts mentions the facts exist in society at that time. During time gap the things get vanished and mixed up with elements of god, but it does not mean nothing was there before that. The dragon , the dinosaurs, the old aged civilization all are mentioned in history books, but it has no proof. There was no Harappa civilization until not discovered under soil of earth. So, science cannot find the facts which have been vanished. The India is land of too much honest and great people. If they have written in books that there was a civilization called Kumari Kumam mens it was there. '

I went to Chennai and other part of Tamilnadu but could not collect any proof, however, old people say with great trust that there was civilization which is now not. It is like reiver Sarswati. The city Allahabad was very famous for the point of three rivers, famously naming Triveni Sangam. The river sarswati vanished but rest of two revers Ganga and Jamuna still flow together.

Thee is no reason of not trusting of our old book. When Veda are oldest most trusted manusceipt on earth, there are many things which facts are recorded but the mode of conveyance was different.

There is need to find the lost universal things mentioned in books of Sanatan religion including Kumari Kundam.

****

CHAPTER - 38

The Anshumati River - The Vedic Confirmation

He Anshumati River, referenced in ancient Indian texts, is traditionally identified with the Yamuna River.

In the Rigveda, the Anshumati is mentioned as the dwelling place of the Asura named Krishna, who resided along its banks with a substantial following. Indra, the Vedic deity, is described as having defeated Krishna and his forces in this region.

The term "Anshumati" also appears in botanical contexts, referring to the plant Desmodium gangeticum, commonly known as sal-leaved desmodium

Today, we delve into the intriguing history of the Anshumati River, a watercourse mentioned in ancient Indian texts, whose exact identity has been a subject of scholarly debate.

The Anshumati River finds mention in the Rigveda, one of the oldest known scriptures. In these hymns, the river is associated with significant events and figures. For instance, Rigveda 8.96.13 describes a figure named Krishna, depicted as an Asura, residing along the banks of the Anshumati with a substantial following. The verse narrates how Indra, a principal deity, identified and defeated Krishna and his forces to protect humanity.

Scholars have attempted to correlate the Anshumati with present-day rivers. A prevailing theory suggests that the Anshumati is an ancient name for the Yamuna River. This identification stems from interpretations of Vedic texts and geographical analyses. The Yamuna, a major tributary of the Ganges, holds substantial significance in Indian culture and history.

Understanding the Anshumati's identity offers insights into the Vedic era's geography and the socio-cultural dynamics of ancient India. Rivers during this period were not merely physical entities but were revered as deities and central to various rituals and narratives. The mention of the Anshumati alongside prominent figures like Indra and Krishna underscores its importance in Vedic traditions.

The exploration of the Anshumati River exemplifies the intricate tapestry of India's historical and cultural evolution. While its exact course may remain uncertain, its legacy persists through the rich literary and spiritual traditions that continue to influence contemporary society.

****

CHAPTER - 39

The Magic

This is a powerful sentence "The science beyond imagination is magic. So never expect magic in life, but be ready to do magic."

Understanding what magic really is. When we hear the word "magic," we often think of illusions, tricks, or supernatural forces. But if we look closely, magic is nothing but science we don't yet understand. Think about it — thousands of years ago, fire was magic. Flying in the sky was magic. Talking to someone across the globe in an instant was magic. Today, all of these things are realities brought to life through science, creativity, and relentless effort.

What seems magical to one generation is normal to the next. The smartphone in your pocket would have been seen as magic a century ago. The power of electricity, the internet, and artificial intelligence are all examples of humans pushing the boundaries of imagination and turning the impossible into reality. This teaches us that magic is not something to wait for — it's something we create through knowledge, innovation, and hard work.

Many of us spend our lives waiting for a miracle. We hope for sudden success, instant wealth, or overnight solutions. But life doesn't work that way. True magic lies in the small, consistent efforts we make every day. Success is not a lightning strike — it's the result of countless sparks of hard work, persistence, and learning.

Every great inventor, artist, leader, or thinker has performed magic. Not with wands, but with their minds, hearts, and hands. They dared to imagine a better world and took action to create it. Being ready to do magic means believing in your potential, embracing challenges, and using the power of knowledge to shape reality.

If you want to perform magic in your life, remember these three principles:

Curiosity: Ask questions. Seek knowledge. The more you learn, the closer you get to unlocking the magic of understanding.

Courage: Don't fear failure. Every failure is a step closer to creating something extraordinary.

Consistency: Small steps, taken consistently, lead to great transformations.

The future belongs to those who don't wait for magic but create it. The next breakthrough, the next innovation, the next great story could come from you. Don't sit back, hoping for miracles. Take action. Learn. Create. Be the magician who turns dreams into reality.

****

CHAPTER - 40

The Pen And The Trust

A powerful moment that we've all experienced but may not have fully understood – the day our teacher gave us a pen instead of a pencil.

At first glance, it may seem like a simple transition. But if you look closely, that pen represents something far greater: trust, responsibility, and confidence.

When we were young, we all started with a pencil. Why? Because mistakes were expected. The eraser was our safety net. But one day, our teacher placed a pen in our hands. In that moment, they silently conveyed a message: "I trust you. I believe you are now capable of writing without fear of mistakes."

The pen symbolizes growth. It means that you've reached a point where your decisions and actions matter. It teaches you to think before you write, to take responsibility for your choices, and to understand that not everything can be erased or undone.

In life, there are no erasers. Once spoken, words can't be taken back. Once a decision is made, its consequences unfold. The pen teaches us mindfulness – the art of being thoughtful and intentional with our actions.

Your teacher trusted you with the pen, just as life and God trust you with the power to shape your own future. This trust is precious. It's a reminder that you are no longer a child scribbling on paper but a creator, writing the chapters of your life with wisdom and courage.

Holding the pen is a responsibility. It means owning up to mistakes instead of erasing them. It means learning from failures and turning them into lessons. In the same way, life expects us to take ownership of our actions. No shortcuts, no excuses — just pure accountability.

The greatest way to honour this trust is to live with integrity. Whether in your personal life, career, or relationships, let every action reflect the wisdom that earned you the right to hold that pen. Be mindful of your words. Stand by your decisions. Take pride in your work.

The next time you hold a pen, remember its silent message. It's not just a tool for writing — it's a symbol of growth, trust, and responsibility. Maintain that trust, not just for your teacher or for God, but for yourself.

Because life isn't about erasing mistakes. It's about writing a story worth remembering.

****

CHAPTER - 41

The Power Of Wisdom And Strength

This is a profound verse from the Ramayana:

"Suksham roop dhari siyahi dikhava, Bheem roop dhari lanka jarava."

This beautiful couplet holds a deep lesson about the responsible use of power. It teaches us that true strength lies not in showing off, but in knowing when to be humble and when to rise with force against injustice.

When Lord Hanuman entered Lanka to find Sita, he took on a subtle, humble form. In front of Sita Mata, he showed compassion and respect, presenting himself in a gentle and reassuring manner. She was in distress, held captive by Ravana, and Hanuman's presence was meant to bring comfort and hope, not fear.

However, when faced with evil – Ravana and his army – Hanuman revealed his immense power. He burned Lanka to the ground, delivering a message that wrongdoers will be met with force and justice.

There is a clear message that true power doesn't lie in constant display but in understanding when to act. Being aggressive or boastful in front of the weak only reveals insecurity, not strength.

Compassion and Strength Go Hand in Hand: In life, there will be moments when we need to show kindness and moments when we must stand firm. The ability to balance both is the hallmark of true character.

Justice Over Domination: Use your abilities to protect, not to dominate. Just as Hanuman's strength was a beacon of justice, our power should be wielded to uphold fairness and protect the vulnerable.

We all must adopt the wisdom of Hanuman. Let our humility comfort those in need, and our strength rise against wrongdoing. Power without control is chaos, but power with wisdom is divine.

****

CHAPTER - 42

Between The Owner And Employee

The Indian education system, while producing millions of graduates and professionals, has largely been focused on creating a workforce for corporates—essentially "corporate laborers." These individuals, despite their immense potential, are often caught in a cycle of following orders, meeting quotas, and maintaining the status quo. However, hidden within this workforce is the ability to innovate, lead, and create something new—a segment that doesn't just follow directions but influences the strategic course of organizations.

It's time for the Indian corporate world to recognize the need for a new segment—one that lies between the traditional roles of owner and employee. This segment would consist of highly skilled advisors with specialized knowledge and a holistic understanding of business. These advisors, acting as part of an independent advisory board, can bridge the gap between ownership and execution, ensuring that decisions are not only effective but also grounded in diverse expertise.

In many ways, this is similar to the jury system in law. A single judge may make biased or flawed decisions due to limited perspectives, but a jury provides collective wisdom, reducing the risk of error. Similarly, corporations need a jury of advisors to navigate the complexities of modern business, ensuring decisions are made with 360-degree insight and minimal risk of failure.

The Need for a "Brain Bank"

India's business landscape is becoming increasingly complex due to the challenges posed by globalization, competition from multinational corporations (MNCs), unionization, lobbying, and other industry-specific hurdles. To meet these challenges, we need more than just effective management. We need a "brain bank"—a group of advisors who are neither employees nor owners but who form the intellectual core of the organization. These advisors would ensure not only profitability but also long-term sustainability and consistent growth.

As Peter Drucker, one of the most influential management thinkers, famously said, "Management is doing things right; leadership is doing the right things." What businesses need now are advisors who can bring leadership and foresight into every decision-making process. This brain bank would help companies make the leap from short-term profits to long-term stability, from crisis management to proactive innovation.

Advisors: Not Employees, Not Owners, But Essential

Advisors would occupy a unique position within the organization. They would not be regular employees tied to operational tasks, nor would they be owners primarily concerned with profit margins and stock prices. Instead, their role would be to provide strategic oversight, ensuring that all decisions are aligned with the company's long-term vision and are sustainable. Their presence could transform how businesses operate, especially in an era where external factors like unions, competition, and market dynamics can drastically impact a company's performance.

This is not a new idea in concept, but its implementation is long overdue in India. Many companies in Silicon Valley, for instance, already have advisory boards that include industry experts, academics, and even former competitors. These advisory boards play a pivotal role in guiding companies through growth phases, market expansions, or crises.

The advisors act much like the mind within the body—overseeing all functions, monitoring health, and making adjustments as necessary. Just as our mind ensures that all bodily systems work in harmony, the advisory board would ensure that all departments within a company—be it finance, operations, HR, or R&D—are working cohesively towards the organization's goals.

Why India Needs This New Segment

India, with its rapidly growing economy, must innovate not just in products and services but also in management structures. As the competition from MNCs increases, it's becoming clear that traditional management hierarchies are insufficient to deal with the complexities of today's business environment. Moreover, unions and lobbying efforts often create hurdles in achieving high performance. As a result, businesses face inefficiencies, slower decision-making, and missed opportunities.

An advisory board made up of experts can address these challenges by bringing in external perspectives, industry best practices, and unbiased advice. Advisors can help identify the gaps that exist in traditional management structures and provide the necessary oversight to ensure these gaps are filled.

As Jack Welch, former CEO of General Electric, once said, "Change before you have to." Indian businesses must adapt to the changing landscape by incorporating this new advisory segment before they are forced to do so by external pressures.

Filling the Gap: Advisors as the Solution

The current system in many Indian businesses is one where directives are given from the top management and are followed by employees. While this might work in a stable environment, it does not account for the dynamic and rapidly evolving challenges businesses face today. There is often no mechanism in place to oversee how well these directives are executed or whether they are even the right directives in the first place.

An advisory board would fill this gap by acting as a layer of oversight, much like how the human mind controls and regulates the functions of the body. Without such a control mechanism, businesses risk making decisions that are reactive rather than proactive, leading to inefficiencies, missed opportunities, and even failure.

"The only sustainable competitive advantage is an organization's ability to learn faster than the competition," said Arie de Geus, a Dutch business theorist. Advisors, with their experience and expertise, can help companies learn faster, innovate better, and navigate challenges more effectively.

Conclusion: The Future of Indian Business

It's time for India to recognize the need for this new segment of advisors, who will not only provide strategic direction but will also ensure that businesses remain competitive in an increasingly complex global market. Advisors are the missing link between owners and employees, offering the wisdom and insight necessary to guide companies through growth, challenges, and transformations.

Incorporating such advisory boards into the fabric of Indian companies will not only help address challenges like unionization and competition but also ensure that businesses are driven by a vision of long-term success. With a focus on creating a 100% performance system and delivering 100% results, this new segment will revolutionize the Indian corporate world, ensuring profitability, stability, and a competitive edge in the global marketplace.

****

CHAPTER - 43

The Teacher

In the grand theatre of life, amidst the clamour of various professions and vocations, there exists a quiet, transformative force—the teacher. A true magician, the teacher does not wield a wand, but their power is far greater: they transform the minds, and more profoundly, the hearts of individuals. They shape our innermost thoughts, stir the depths of our emotions, and light the torch of wisdom that guides us through life's darkest paths. A teacher's magic is subtle yet eternal, casting spells of knowledge and compassion that linger within us forever.

As Ralph Waldo Emerson once remarked, "The mind, once stretched by a new idea, never returns to its original dimensions." The teacher, in this sense, is the magician who stretches our minds and alters our hearts, leaving us forever changed.

A teacher's role in the world is not just to fill the minds of students with facts and figures. Rather, the true work of a teacher is akin to that of a sculptor, patiently chipping away at the rough edges of ignorance, fear, and doubt, revealing the polished potential within every individual. Like Michelangelo seeing the angel in the marble, the teacher recognizes the inherent beauty and capacity in each soul, no matter how hidden.

In literature, great teachers are often depicted as figures who understand the deeper purpose of education. In To Kill a Mockingbird, Attics Finch, a moral guide and father figure, teaches his children the importance of empathy, truth, and justice. His teachings go beyond textbooks and enter the realm of ethical wisdom. Similarly, in The Karate

Kid, Mr. Miyagi's lessons about patience, balance, and perseverance serve as metaphors for life itself. These teachers do not merely transfer knowledge; they transform character.

The essence of a great teacher lies not in the curriculum they follow, but in the way they shape the heart and spirit of their students, equipping them to confront the world with courage, kindness, and integrity.

The relationship between a teacher and their student is a sacred one, steeped in trust and respect. It is within this dynamic that the most profound transformations occur. Knowledge, while important, is secondary to the emotional and spiritual change a teacher can ignite. When a teacher truly cares, they do not just impart lessons; they inspire their students to believe in themselves, to see the world in new ways, and to reach for heights they never imagined possible.

A great teacher teaches students how to think, not what to think. This is the essence of Socratic wisdom—posing questions that awaken the soul and open the heart to new possibilities. In the Platonic dialogues, Socrates serves as the ideal model of a teacher. He doesn't fill his students with answers but draws the truth out of them, leading them to self-realization.

Similarly, the poet William Butler Yeats famously said, "Education is not the filling of a pail, but the lighting of a fire." The fire that a teacher ignites in the heart of a student is the flame of curiosity, passion, and purpose. This flame, once kindled, grows into a beacon that guides a student throughout life, much like a lighthouse that leads a ship through treacherous waters.

The magic of a teacher lies not only in their ability to impart intellectual knowledge but also in their capacity to navigate the emotional landscapes of their students. Many of us have experienced moments when a teacher's belief in us became the foundation upon which we built our self-confidence and resilience. In the hands of a gifted teacher, education becomes emotional alchemy, a process by which raw potential is refined into shining gold.

Consider the example of Professor Dumbledore in Harry Potter, whose understanding of the emotional and moral struggles of his students—particularly Harry—sets him apart as a guide and mentor. Dumbledore's greatest lessons were not in spells or potions, but in teaching Harry how to confront fear, loss, and love. His wisdom lay in his ability to see Harry's heart and to nurture it with compassion and insight.

In the realm of real life, there are countless stories of teachers who have changed lives not by being academically brilliant, but by offering kindness, patience, and empathy. Teachers become life guides, helping students navigate personal struggles, self-doubt, and social pressures. Their greatest gift is often the simple yet profound act of listening—of making their students feel seen, heard, and valued.

The true magic of a teacher is that their influence never fades. Long after the lessons are forgotten, the emotional and spiritual imprint remains. A teacher's words, encouragement, and belief in their students echo through the years, influencing not only the individual but also those around them. A great teacher creates a ripple effect, spreading wisdom and compassion far beyond the classroom.

Leo Buscaglia, a well-known professor and motivational speaker, shared in his works how a teacher's love and encouragement had profoundly shaped his life. He often emphasized the human touch in teaching—the importance of caring deeply for students as individuals. "Too often we underestimate the power of a touch, a smile, a kind word, a listening ear, or the smallest act of caring, all of which have the potential to turn a life around," Buscaglia wrote.

The lasting impact of teachers can be seen in the lives of their students, many of whom go on to become teachers themselves, continuing the cycle of transformation. Each generation of students carries forward the wisdom of their teachers, passing it down like a precious heirloom, adding to it their own experiences and insights.

In the final analysis, the greatest gift of a teacher is not the knowledge they impart, but the empowerment they offer. By teaching students to think critically, to trust in their abilities, and to open their hearts to the world, teachers create magicians out of their students. These students, in turn, go forth into the world, spreading light, knowledge, and compassion.

In the words of Carl Jung, "One looks back with appreciation to the brilliant teachers, but with gratitude to those who touched our human feelings. The curriculum is so much necessary raw material, but warmth is the vital element for the growing plant and for the soul of the child."

The teacher's legacy is not simply in the minds they have shaped but in the hearts they have touched. They are the silent magicians, working wonders that last far beyond their years, transforming the world one heart at a time.

The magic of teaching is infinite, boundless, and timeless. It reaches across generations, cultures, and experiences, always serving as a guiding force in the shaping of individuals and societies. While the world often celebrates material achievements and outward success, the quiet, transformative work of teachers—the magicians of the heart—remains one of the most powerful forces in human history.

A teacher does not just impart knowledge. They open the gates to self-discovery, ethical understanding, and emotional growth. Their magic lies in their ability to change lives, to turn doubt into belief, and to fill hearts with the courage to face the world. In this way, the teacher is, and will always be, the greatest magician of all.

****

CHAPTER - 44

The War Without Weapon

Throughout human history, wars have been fought with weapons, bloodshed, and destruction. Kingdoms have risen and fallen, leaving behind ruins and sorrow. However, the greatest revolution in history was not led by swords or guns but by an unbreakable spirit of nonviolence. Mahatma Gandhi, the father of the Indian nation, pioneered a form of resistance that changed the course of history—Ahinsa (Nonviolence). This method became the ultimate weapon in India's struggle for freedom, proving that moral strength and unwavering faith could defeat even the mightiest of empires.

Ahimsa, derived from Sanskrit, means "non-harm" or "nonviolence." Gandhi's belief in this principle was rooted in ancient Indian philosophy, especially in Jainism, Buddhism, and Hinduism. It was not just about refraining from physical violence but about eradicating hatred, anger, and oppression. Ahinsa required immense courage, patience, and self-discipline, as it sought to win over the oppressor with love and truth rather than with force.

India had been under British rule for nearly two centuries, suffering from economic exploitation, political subjugation, and social oppression. The conventional method of armed resistance had been tried but was brutally suppressed by the British. It was at this critical moment that Mahatma Gandhi introduced Satyagraha—the principle of nonviolent resistance, a strategy that combined truth, civil disobedience, and non-cooperation.

One of the most iconic moments in the history of Ahinsa was the Salt March of 1930. The British had imposed heavy taxes on salt, an essential commodity for Indians. Gandhi led thousands of people on a 240-mile march to the Arabian Sea, where they made salt in defiance of the British law. This simple yet powerful act of nonviolent defiance ignited a nationwide movement, proving that the British could be challenged without lifting a single weapon.

Gandhi urged Indians to boycott British goods, institutions, and services. Millions of Indians refused to pay taxes, left government jobs, and abandoned British-made products. This widespread non-cooperation movement weakened the economic and administrative grip of the British. When the British government responded with violence and mass arrests, Gandhi and his followers endured it with patience, demonstrating the moral superiority of their cause.

Gandhi's philosophy of nonviolence did not just free India; it became an inspiration for global movements. Leaders like Martin Luther King Jr. in the United States and Nelson Mandela in South Africa adopted similar nonviolent methods to fight racial discrimination and apartheid. Ahinsa became a universal weapon for oppressed communities across the world, proving that even the most powerful regimes could be challenged through peace and moral strength.

The war without weapons led by Mahatma Gandhi remains one of the most extraordinary events in world history. It was a battle won not with armies, but with determination, self-sacrifice, and truth. Today, in a world still plagued by violence and conflict, the principles of Ahimsa serve as a timeless lesson—that true power lies not in destruction but in peace, love, and justice.

The success of Ahinsa proves that even the mightiest oppressors can be brought to their knees without a drop of blood being shed. It is not just a strategy but a way of life, a force greater than any weapon, and a beacon of hope for future generations.

****

CHAPTER - 45

Dhava

The ancient Vedas, particularly the Rig Veda, contain intriguing references to a celestial body known as Dhava, described as a planet with conditions similar to Earth. It is often portrayed as a larger and more advanced world, supporting life and civilization. According to Vedic texts (as referenced in Ved – Decoding the Mystery of the Universe), Dhava was a father planet, while Earth was considered the mother planet due to its smaller size and dependence on solar energy.

Vedic scriptures mention that sunlight travelled from Earth to Dhava, forming a radiant bridge. This implies that Dhava was either near Earth or directly observable from ancient times. The descriptions of rains, rivers, agriculture, flora, fauna, and human-like beings suggest a thriving ecosystem similar to Earth's.

Locating Dhava in the Solar System :

If we analyze our planetary system, the sequence from the Sun is:

- Mercury
- Venus
- Earth
- Mars
- Jupiter
- Saturn

- Uranus
- Neptune

The Vedic assertion that sunlight travelled between Earth and Dhava suggests that Dhava could be located between Earth and Mars or Mars itself may have been referred to as Dhava in ancient times. Modern astronomical studies have shown evidence that Mars once had liquid water, rivers, and possibly even life. This aligns with the Vedic description of Dhava, strengthening the hypothesis that Mars was an ancient habitable world.

Scientific Evidence Supporting the Existence of Dhava

Evidence of Water on Mars:

NASA's Curiosity and Perseverance rovers have found sedimentary deposits that suggest past rivers, lakes, and an ocean.

Water-ice deposits have been confirmed beneath the Martian surface, indicating the planet may have had Earth-like conditions in the past.

Possibility of Ancient Civilizations:

Unusual geological formations on Mars, resembling structures similar to Earth's pyramids and temples, have led to speculation about past intelligent life.

Some scientists suggest that if life did exist on Mars, it may have migrated to another planet (possibly Earth or another undiscovered body).

Interstellar Migration Hypothesis:

Just as modern space agencies explore colonization on Mars, it is conceivable that ancient civilizations migrated from Mars (Dhava) to Earth after catastrophic climate changes.

The Vedic assertion that humanity was once located in the Saptrishi Constellation before arriving on Earth suggests the possibility of advanced interstellar migration.

The Future of Dhava Exploration

Given its historical and mythological significance, exploring Dhava should be a major focus of space research. Potential research avenues include:

Further Mars exploration missions to confirm past habitability.

Search for exoplanets within the Sun's gravitational influence that may have Dhava-like properties.

Deep space telescopic studies to locate any celestial body matching Dhava's description.

AI-driven Vedic translation projects to decode and interpret lost astronomical knowledge from ancient texts.

The concept of Dhava as the nearest habitable planet to Earth holds immense scientific and philosophical significance. Whether it was an ancient reference to Mars or an undiscovered celestial body, Dhava represents humanity's quest for knowledge, exploration, and survival beyond Earth. Future research may one day confirm the existence of this mythical yet scientifically plausible world, opening doors to interplanetary colonization and the rediscovery of lost cosmic wisdom.

This document presents a professional and research-driven discussion on Dhava, integrating ancient Vedic knowledge with modern scientific theories. There is need to understand of contents of Ved which have deep cosmic wisdom.

****

CHAPTER - 46

Cosmic Wisdom

The universe operates with an unwavering discipline, a rhythm so precise that even the most advanced human systems pale in comparison. Each morning, the sun rises without fail, returning to its position in our sky because the Earth rotates at a staggering speed of 1,670 km per hour, completing a full revolution of 40,080 km every day. This cosmic mechanism ensures the continuity of life, demonstrating the universe's impeccable order and commitment to balance.

This celestial precision is not an accident; it is a message—one that underscores the fundamental principles of discipline, duty, and persistence. The universe does not waver, does not rest, and does not falter in its duties. The sun does not rise late, and the planets do not stray from their orbits. This is a lesson for humanity: if the cosmos, which is infinitely more complex and vast, can function with such harmony, then so can we. Though humans may not possess the sheer power of the sun, we are endowed with intelligence, awareness, and the ability to lead disciplined lives.

Discipline is not merely about following routines, it is about maintaining a mental ecosystem free from the disruptive forces of negativity. Just as cosmic forces regulate planetary movements, we must regulate our thoughts, actions, and intentions. A disciplined mind resists the distractions of doubt, fear, and selfish desires, instead fostering a culture of selflessness, purpose, and service. The universe provides unconditionally—it does not trade sunlight for rewards, nor does it demand compensation for the air we breathe or the soil that nourishes us.

This cosmic generosity extends an invitation to humanity to give without expecting in return, to serve without the calculation of profit and loss, and to nurture without the expectation of immediate results. If we attune ourselves to these messages, we can transcend beyond our material limitations and align with a higher cosmic order.

From a scientific perspective, our solar system is an intricate design of gravitational interdependence. Each planetary motion, each rotation, and each revolution contributes to a larger purpose—the sustenance of life and the continuity of cosmic balance. Life on Earth is not merely a random occurrence but a finely tuned orchestration of forces that have been meticulously aligned over billions of years.

The very existence of our planet, its fertile soil, its renewable cycles of water and energy, and its capacity for regrowth, is a testament to the cosmic intelligence at play. If we choose to align with these natural principles—embracing sustainability, self-discipline, and respect for the resources given to us—we can unlock an evolutionary pathway that leads us to our next great destination.

The cosmos does not limit us. The vastness of space hints at infinite possibilities, and the potential for human civilization to expand beyond Earth remains a real scientific pursuit. If we learn from the messages encoded in the structure of the universe, if we mimic the discipline of celestial bodies and the generosity of cosmic forces, then we may one day traverse the stars, reaching beyond Earth to find new homes in the vast expanse of the cosmos.

The key to this future lies not in technological advancements alone but in understanding and adopting the cosmic principles that have governed existence for eons. The discipline of the universe, the selflessness of nature, and the unwavering persistence of celestial bodies—all these are lessons that, if internalized, will guide humanity toward a brighter, more sustainable future.

By aligning our lives with the messages of the cosmos, we can transcend the mundane and elevate our existence, paving the way for a journey far beyond our current reality. Listen carefully what Cosmic Powers are trying to tell us.

****

CHAPTER - 47

Health

"The biggest problem on Earth is health—not just physical health, but also mental health, cultural health, language, character, actions, humanity, and climate.

Health of Language - Abusive language is now used openly. Films and TV serials approved by government authorities often contain harsh and offensive language. Simply displaying a warning that a show contains strong language does not serve any purpose—it is still being broadcast into every home, where children are exposed to it. Language is connected to the mind and reflects the polluted thinking of people in media and government.

Not only news channels but also print media use inappropriate words. For example, if a team wins a match, the media might write, 'Team A brutally destroyed Team B,' as if describing a war or crime. Instead of simply stating, 'Team A won the match with great playing,' they exaggerate events for dramatic effect. Unfortunately, good words are no longer preferred by the public—sensationalism is demanded."

Health of Religion - The fastest decline in health is in Dharma and religion. Dharma and religion were created to uphold the highest level of humanity among all, but today, they are being used to demonstrate power. Dharma has become a display of strength and politics. People have forgotten the true meaning and purpose of Dharma.

Religion and Dharma should be acts of humanity practiced from the heart and within the home, but they have now moved to the streets. Worship is being conducted on roads merely to gather crowds and showcase power. Religion should reside in the heart and be reflected in our actions.

Dharma is not about making a spectacle and showing it to the public—it should be adopted in karma (actions) to build a character as righteous as that of our Gods.

Mental Pollution - People who wear kilos of chandan (sandalwood paste) and kumkum (vermillion) on their faces, portraying themselves as representatives of God, often use the most polluted and hateful language. Educated individuals—teachers, leaders, saints, and youth—have become increasingly focused on money and selfishness.

Earlier, unethical practices were mostly associated with the poor, who were forced to adopt them for survival. However, very surprisingly, this corruption has now spread to the educated and literate. When a government officer demands a bribe, it is a sign of mental illness. Similarly, when a doctor forces unnecessary surgeries and expenses, or when a leader sells out the country and damages its future, it is evidence of moral degradation.

India is deeply trapped in this crisis. There are endless incidents proving that corruption has become a way of life rather than a crime. If a judge takes a bribe to give a biased judgment, if a police officer takes a bribe to hide a crime, or if a leader harms the nation for personal gain, it is proof that India has lost the glory of Buddha, Vivekananda, Rama, Krishna, Gandhi, and, lastly, Dr. A.P.J. Abdul Kalam.

Character - When we talk about character, it rarely matches that of legends. A literate person holding prestigious positions such as IAS, PCS, Bank Officer, or Police Officer often demands more dowery (bribe) in weddings, justifying it by their high status and wealth. A financially well-off person, who should support a poor girl with good character, instead demands a higher dowry. This essentially means he sells his position to the girl's father.

Such practices have created a situation in India where girls are seen as a burden on families, leading to the tragic reality of female infanticide. Is this the same Hindu nation where people claim to pray more than they eat, but not for public welfare—only for their own personal gains?

Even when it comes to something as sacred as blood donation, which is meant to save lives, people do not donate unless they receive something in return. Yet, when they require blood at a hospital, they have to purchase it with money.

Society has lost its character. People have created a web of selfish practices, where their only goal is to exploit and take from others—whether through the fear of karma, misuse of religion, abuse of power, or emotional manipulation.

This country has great examples of Mahatma Gandhi, who sacrificed his life for the nation despite belonging to a wealthy family. There is also Saint Dadhichi, who gave up his life to donate his bones, which were used to create a weapon to destroy demons. Lord Indra forged the Vajra from his bones, through which all demons were ultimately defeated.

In fact, after independence, two generations have passed. The third generation, now enjoying a comfortable life, has no knowledge of the sacrifices made to achieve independence and develop the country. When India gained independence, it had ₹400 crore in rural debt and was at ground level in terms of development. The country broke free after 400 years of Mughal rule and 300 years of British rule, leaving it in a state of extreme poverty.

The true heroes built a strong army, rockets, ISRO, AIIMS, public corporations, and industries. Women, who were once victims of Sati, are now excelling in multinational and national software companies, working in five-star office environments.

The generations who witnessed or listened carefully to stories of poverty, Mughal and British oppression, and the struggle for independence have passed away. The third generation, having received everything effortlessly, now lives in a comfort zone, showing little respect for elders and their sacrifices. They prioritize religion, hatred, and money over ethics and values. Honesty has become an obsolete word, and the concept of sacrifice has vanished from their vocabulary.

India must change itself, or soon, people will start questioning who rules them. If corruption persists, foreign rulers may seem preferable to our failing system, and we could once again lose control of our nation.

Change it or face it—the choice is in the hands of the youth, who must step up and take charge of the country's future.

****

CHAPTER - 48

The Purity Within

Purify your body and soul to such an extent that when you stand in a river, the river itself transforms into the holy Ganga, adopting your purity. This metaphor emphasizes the power of internal sanctity, suggesting that true purity lies within us and not in external rituals. Many believe that a dip in the holy Ganga can cleanse one's sins, but why commit sins in the first place? Why should we rely on external means or divine forgiveness to rectify the wrongs we have done? Instead, we should strive to embody a life so virtuous that we become an example for others to follow.

The Illusion of Washing away sins

The notion that sins can be washed away by bathing in sacred rivers reflects a misunderstanding of spiritual principles. True cleansing is not about immersing the body in holy waters but about transforming the mind and heart. It is about cultivating a character that aligns with the highest ideals of humanity. The question we must ask ourselves is not, "How do I cleanse myself of sins?" but rather, "How do I avoid committing sins at all?"

Living as a Shadow of Divinity

The ultimate aspiration should not be to merely seek forgiveness but to live as a reflection of divine qualities—compassion, honesty, and righteousness. We may not become God, but we can strive to be a shadow of divinity, an embodiment of principles that protect and uplift humanity. Figures like Lord Buddha and Swami Vivekananda stand as timeless examples of this ideal. They did not seek purification through rituals but through a life of integrity, service, and enlightenment.

A Call to Action

Let us focus on nurturing our inner purity and integrity. Instead of being among those who seek to wash away sins, let us aim to be those whose very presence inspires others. Let us work toward being protectors and guides, fostering a world where goodness and humanity prevail.

This message invites introspection and transformation, urging us to redefine purity as an internal state rather than an external ritual. In doing so, we not only elevate ourselves but also contribute to a more compassionate and virtuous world.

****

CHAPTER - 49

Uttarayan And Dakshinayan

Makar Sankranti, commonly associated with Uttarayan, marks a significant astronomical transition where the Sun moves from Sagittarius (Dhanu Rashi) to Capricorn (Makara Rashi) in the celestial sphere. This festival, deeply rooted in Hindu traditions, celebrates the Sun's northward movement—an event with both scientific and cultural significance. Uttarayan symbolizes the onset of longer days and increased solar energy, while Dakshinayan represents the Sun's southward journey, characterized by shorter days and a decrease in solar intensity.

Astronomical Context

The Earth's tilt and its elliptical orbit around the Sun lead to variations in solar energy received across hemispheres. During Dakshinayan, from the Summer Solstice (around June 21) to the Winter Solstice (around December 21), the Sun appears to move southward. Conversely, Uttarayan begins post-Winter Solstice and culminates with longer days as the Sun shifts northward. This movement is linked to the Sun's relative position with respect to the Tropics of Cancer and Capricorn.

Energy Dynamics: Sunlight's Influence Dakshinayan (June 21–December 21):

The Sun's energy diminishes as its angle decreases. Nights grow longer, leading to cooler temperatures. Extended darkness facilitates conditions favorable for microbial growth, often resulting in increased susceptibility to diseases, particularly during the monsoon season.

The Period Symbolizes Rest And Conservation In Nature. Uttarayan (December 21–June 21):

Solar energy intensifies, enhancing life processes and agricultural activities.

Longer daylight hours reduce microbial activity, leading to better health conditions.

This period is traditionally associated with productivity and vitality, often perceived as auspicious in Indian culture.

Cultural Interpretation Of Cosmic Phenomena

In ancient times, when scientific understanding was limited, these solar movements were personified through myths and rituals. The Sun's journey was linked to divine forces, encouraging people to celebrate its transitions. These festivals served as a way to impart knowledge of cosmic phenomena while fostering community and spiritual connection.

Balancing Energy: A Scientific Perspective

While Uttarayan is associated with prosperity due to increased solar energy, it is essential to note that an excess of energy can also lead to environmental imbalances, such as heatwaves. Conversely, Dakshinayan, despite its challenges, allows ecosystems to recover and prepare for growth during the next cycle.

Festivals And Astronomical Awareness

Indian festivals, like Makar Sankranti, often represent pivotal astronomical events. Initially, humans may have linked these occurrences to deities for ease of understanding. Over time, as scientific awareness grew, it became evident that these traditions were rooted in cosmic phenomena, underscoring the importance of solar energy in sustaining life on Earth.

By appreciating the scientific basis behind such celebrations, we can foster a deeper understanding of their relevance while honoring the wisdom of ancient civilizations.

****

CHAPTER - 50

Holi - The Solar System

As are customary of the festival of color, the 25th of March or Holi falls on a full moon day, when the moon is in Leo, representing fire. However, the moon is not affected negatively, because the Sun is in Aquarius at the same time

During the festival of Holi, the Sun is in the Purva Bhadrapada constellation of Aquarius, and the Moon is in the Purva Phalguni constellation of Leo.

Holi is a lunar festival that takes place during the full moon in the month of Phalguna. The Sun's light is said to destroy evil energies and transform them into positive ones. The Moon in Leo represents fire.

Jupiter is considered the nakshatra lord of the Sun, and Venus is considered the nakshatra lord of the Moon.

Holi is a festival of colors that marks the beginning of spring. It is celebrated throughout the Indian subcontinent and represents the victory of good over evil.

On the day of Holi, astrologers believe that the Sun and the Moon are on opposite ends of each other in the sky. From an astrological perspective, this position is considered to be a favorable time. During this time, the Moon lies in the house of Leo and Virgo, while the Sun is placed in Aquarius and Pisces. Rahu often transits into Sagittarius.

As a story, a son named, Prahlad was later born to Hiranyakashyap. Much to Hiranyakashyap's dismay, Prahlad grew up to become a staunch devotee of Lord Vishnu. Hiranyakashipu was enraged by this act of defiance and he commanded Prahlad's sister, Holika to kill Prahlad by taking him into a fire. Holika herself was immune to the effects of fire, by virtue of the blessings that she was bestowed.

In the event, Holika went through with the plan, however Lord Vishnu's grace led to Prahlad emerging unscathed, while Holika was burnt to ashes. The legend of Prahlad and Holika thus lives on in the form of the festival of Holi.

Here a message was given by Devas to us that After the day of Holi there will be a great heat. The heat will not affect to good person but will kill to bad person like Holika. Even though Holika was immune from the effect of fire but her wrongfulness forced God to withdraw the immune system resulting she was burnt. There is clear message to stay with rightfulness The universe is watching and will take appropriate decision at right time. Even if some one has great power or immune system, will not be leave from punishment if is wrong or trying to kill rightfulness.

This festival has significant role of messaging to human civilization living in land of India.

The other story of lord Krishna and Radha has also a great message for us. Due to colour difference between lord Krishna and love Radha there was problem in marriage. The throwing of colours on each other means every one should have all colours. The colours represents to different type of happiness so all should have all happiness. If some one has extra colours and happiness give it to others who don't have and all people should have the same colours.

Scientifically, celebrating this festival has more than one benefit. The bright colors and flowers seen during Holi can stimulate the human body to renew and regenerate itself. Playing with different colours can treat our bodies for what it lacks. For instance, the color green stands for new beginnings, while yellow stands for joy and pink for love. The color red represents fertility and orange represents life itself. The color purple could refer to new possibilities. Color powder or gulal is said to have a medicinal significance as the colors are traditionally made from Kumkum, Bilva, Neem, and other medicinal herbs that have been suggested by Ayurvedic practitioners. Colors are derived from plants like sandalwood, mehendi, haldi, berries, tea leaves, and beetroot.

Also, Holi occurs during the winter-spring transformation period, during which bacteria grow both in the environment and the body. A day before the celebration, the temperature starts turning quite hot. The heat from the Holika Dahan destroys the bacteria in the body and fully cleanses it when the Parikrama (circling the fire) is completed.

From commemorating the bounty of spring to acknowledging a good harvest and taking part in the abundance of nature, Holi tops the list as a festival that is significant even today. The best takeaways from this festival are the insistence on resetting and renewing relationships, doing away with evil, and seeing the good in everyone and everything.

****

CHAPTER - 51

Education

Education is the cornerstone of any thriving society. It has the transformative power to elevate individuals from ordinary to extraordinary by imparting knowledge, fostering critical thinking, and nurturing innovation. However, when access to education becomes so prohibitively expensive that individuals must resort to taking education loans or sacrificing their entire income, it raises a serious question about the civilization and ethics of the society in which we live.

The Price of Knowledge

In a truly civilized society, education should not be a privilege reserved for the wealthy but a fundamental right accessible to all. When education costs escalate beyond the reach of ordinary citizens, it creates a system where inequality is perpetuated. Families are forced into debt cycles to afford quality education, and individuals begin their professional lives burdened by financial obligations. This not only stifles their growth but also inhibits their contribution to the broader economy.

Degrees Without Value

An even graver concern arises when, despite obtaining expensive degrees, individuals find themselves unemployed. In such scenarios, the degree loses its essence and becomes no more than a piece of paper. This situation reflects a systemic failure: an education system that neither aligns with job market demands nor equips students with practical skills.

Such an outcome exposes the inefficiency and inadequacy of the system, highlighting its inability to deliver on its promises.

Education as a National Investment

If a nation aspires to secure a bright future, it must prioritize free and accessible education. Countries that provide cost-free education recognize it as an investment in human capital. They understand that an educated populace drives innovation, enhances productivity, and fosters social harmony. Education should not be seen as a commodity to be purchased but as a public good that benefits society at large.

A Civilized Society's Responsibility

A truly advanced and ethical society would ensure that every citizen has access to quality education without financial barriers. Such a system would produce skilled individuals ready to contribute meaningfully to the country's development. If education remains unaffordable, it is a clear indication of an exploitative system where those in power prioritize personal gains over societal well-being.

To create a great nation with a promising future, governments and policymakers must commit to providing cost-free, high-quality education. This requires rethinking budget allocations, eliminating corruption, and fostering partnerships between public and private sectors. Education is not just an individual's pathway to success; it is the foundation of a prosperous and equitable society.

If education in your country is expensive and inaccessible, it is a stark warning. It indicates that the leadership may not have the people's best interests at heart, making them adversaries rather than allies in the journey toward progress. The time to act is now—for education is not just a right; it is the lifeline of civilization.

****

CHAPTER - 52

The Lessons From History

The Mughal Empire, once boasting the largest and most formidable army on Earth between 1528 and 1750, was ultimately defeated by the British. Despite their dominance, the British Empire, too, faced expulsion from India, but not through war. Instead, a non-violent Congress, without an army, compelled them to leave. These historical events invite us to ponder the dynamics of power, rule, and the essence of governance.

The Decline of the Mughals

The Mughals, despite their might, failed to fully integrate with the Indian populace. Their inability to embrace Indian culture and ethos created a divide, fostering resentment among the local population. This lack of acceptance made the British appear more favourable, leading many Indians to support them over the Mughals. Consequently, the Mughal Empire crumbled, paving the way for British dominance.

The British Era and Its Consequences

The British, though technologically advanced and administratively efficient, were exploitative rulers. They looted India, transferring immense wealth, including treasures like the Kohinoor diamond, to Britain. Their welfare initiatives for Indians were minimal, and their policies often humiliated the native populace. Over time, the disdain and disrespect they showed towards Indians became their undoing. The unity fostered by the struggle for independence, coupled with the sacrifices of countless freedom fighters, forced the British to retreat.

The Internal Struggles of India

Before the advent of the Mughals and British, India was plagued by deep caste divisions. The upper castes often oppressed the lower castes, subjecting them to a life of servitude. This systemic inequality created an environment ripe for exploitation by foreign powers. When the Mughals arrived, they offered the oppressed an alternative, leading many to favor them over their own rulers. The failure of Indian rulers to unite and treat their people with dignity and fairness was a significant factor in India's susceptibility to external domination.

A Lesson from Lord Ram

History teaches us that sustainable rule is rooted in justice, empathy, and inclusivity. Lord Ram's reign, often cited as an ideal, lasted for 26,000 years (as per mythological references). His governance was characterized by compassion for all, protection of the vulnerable, and a deep understanding of his people's needs. This legacy stands in stark contrast to the exploitation and divisiveness of the Mughals and British.

Contemporary Parallels

Today, the shadows of past rulers linger. Many political leaders treat governance as a privilege rather than a responsibility, living lavishly while their people suffer. Poverty deepens, inequality widens, and the gap between the rich and the poor grows insurmountable. Such conditions mirror the eras of Mughal and British rule, signaling the potential for history to repeat itself if unchecked.

A Call to Action

The choice before us is clear. Do we emulate the Mughals, outsiders who failed to unite with their people? Do we mirror the British, looters who disregarded the welfare of the land they ruled? Do we perpetuate the caste-based inequalities of pre-Mughal India? Or do we aspire to the ideals of Lord Ram, a leader who ruled with fairness, love, and justice?

The future of our society depends on this decision. It is a call to reject divisiveness, exploitation, and inequality and to embrace unity, compassion, and progress for all. As citizens, we must demand accountability and humanity from our leaders, ensuring that governance is a service, not a privilege.

Let us learn from history, not repeat its mistakes. The choice is ours.

****

CHAPTER - 53

The Cosmic Arsenal: Ancient Indian Insights Into Solar Materials For Divine Weapons

In ancient Indian scriptures, particularly in Puranas, there is a fascinating account of Lord Vishwakarma, a revered architect, crafting three divine articles from the material of the Sun - the Sudarshan Chakra, a divine weapon; the Trishul of Lord Shiva, another formidable weapon; and the Pushpak Viman, an extraordinary aircraft. All these three powerful artifacts forged from the material of the Sun – suggests capabilities far beyond conventional comprehension. According to Vedic wisdom, these divine creations possessed the potential to either dismantle malevolent civilizations or transport masses to distant corners of the universe. The narrative of human civilization shifting from the SaptRishi Mandal further adds a layer of intrigue to the profound possibilities embedded in these celestial creations. These celestial creations include Exploring these ancient texts reveals a profound understanding of harnessing solar materials for advanced technological applications.

1. Sudarshan Chakra: Unveiling the Power of Solar Energy

The Sudarshan Chakra, a mystical discus with potent capabilities, is said to have been crafted from the material of the Sun. This raises intriguing questions about the utilization of solar energy in weaponry. The ancient texts imply the possibility of crafting weapons not from conventional materials but from the powerful energies associated with the Sun. It suggests a paradigm beyond traditional manufacturing, akin to the utilization of energy for creation. The Sudarshcan Chakra was weapon which had power to destroy anything. There was no weapon in universe which can destroy it.

2. **Trishul of Lord Shiva: A Divine Trident Linked to Solar Forces**

The Trishul, a symbol of Lord Shiva's power, is another divine weapon created from the material of the Sun. Its association with solar materials hints at a profound connection between advanced weaponry and celestial energies. The synchronization of power at the point of the trident showcases a level of technological sophistication that goes beyond conventional understanding. An another unbeatable weapon crafted for another superpower - lord Shiva.

3. **Pushpak Viman: Solar-Powered Cosmic Conveyance**

The Pushpak Viman, an aircraft propelled by solar materials, presents a marvel of ancient aerospace engineering. With the ability to transport masses to any corner of the universe, this celestial vehicle hints at a level of technological sophistication transcending earthly limitations. The notion of shifting human civilization from the Sapt Rishi Mandal echoes the idea of interplanetary exploration facilitated by solar-powered means. This ancient concept beckons scientists to explore the possibilities of harnessing solar energy for advanced aerospace applications. The Pushpak Viman had power to go in seconds in any part of universe. It had unlimited capacity to sit. Lord ram went to heaven on this aircraft only.

Vedic Insights on Human Civilization's Migration:

The Vedic assertion of human civilization shifting from the Sapt Rishi Mandal introduces a fascinating perspective on ancient spacefaring endeavors. It suggests that the divine artifacts were not merely instruments of destruction but also vehicles for transcendence, capable of carrying humanity to new realms in the vast expanse of the universe.

Ancient Wisdom for Modern Innovation:

The power of the Sun, a force that has illuminated our planet for millions of years, holds untapped potential for technological advancements. Ancient Indian scriptures provide glimpses into a realm where divine weapons and aircraft were crafted from solar materials. This prompts a re-evaluation of our understanding of materials and energy sources, urging scientists to explore innovative approaches inspired by ancient wisdom for the betterment of humanity.

The three divine artifacts, rooted in the material of the Sun, paint a picture of an ancient civilization endowed with cosmic prowess. Beyond their potential for destruction, these celestial creations signify a nuanced understanding of harnessing solar energy for benevolent purposes, such as transportation and the safeguarding of civilizations. Exploring these narratives invites us to reevaluate our perception of ancient technologies and consider the profound possibilities that lie at the intersection of divine wisdom and advanced cosmic engineering. The idea of using materials from the Sun, with its immense power and energy, poses a revolutionary concept for contemporary scientists. As we grapple with the challenges of nuclear power on Earth, exploring alternative and sustainable energy sources inspired by ancient insights could pave the way for a more harmonious and technologically advanced future.

****

RAMAYANA THE ABSTRACT AND THE MEANING

CHAPTER - 54

Sundar Kand Chhand

Chhand: *Pratham Pranam Keenhi Siru Naai, Baithe Puni Tat Darbh Dasai*

Meaning: Lord Ram first bowed his head and offered his respects to the ocean. Then he sat down on the shore after spreading some kusha grass.

Establishing the Religious Constitution of Sanatan - Humility:

Lord Ram asked the ocean deity for a path to Lanka, but the ocean, in its obstinacy, did not grant him a way. All the monkeys prayed to Lord Ram that he could dry up the ocean with a single arrow, which would give them a path. However, Lord Ram adhered to the principles of dharma. Through his actions, he inscribed in the constitution that one should first approach with humility. If one needs to ask for something, it should be done with respect and decorum. Therefore, being the avatar of Shri Hari Vishnu, Lord Ram bowed to the ocean and, to receive the ocean deity's response, sat down on the ground after spreading kusha grass.

This incident is a part of the Sanatan Dharma's constitution, which emphasizes that one should always act with humility. If something needs to be asked, it should be requested with a bowed head and humility. Even if people provoke, one should not lose temper but follow wisdom and the religious constitution. Power should not be used until it is absolutely necessary or when no other option remains.

This significant fact mentioned in Shri Ramayana serves as a lesson and guideline for our new generation, for the youth, and for the people of India. If you follow Sanatan Dharma, make humility your companion. Do not misuse power, and do not try to take anything by force. The primary duty is to request with humility.

****

CHAPTER - 55

Lankakand

Chhand: *Ram Dut Main Matu Janaki, Satya Sapath Karuna Nidhan Ki*

Meaning: (Hanuman Ji said), "O Mother Janaki, I am the messenger of Lord Ram. I swear by the compassion incarnate (Lord Ram)."

Sanatan Constitution - Your Identity is Defined by Your Elders:

Hanuman Ji very humbly said to Mother Janaki, "O Mother, I am the messenger of Lord Ram." Hanuman Ji was the son of the wind god (Vayu). He was blessed by the gods and was immensely powerful. However, he introduced himself as the messenger of Lord Ram. The Sanatan constitution states that your identity is defined by those great beings who have established you in that form. Hanuman Ji was a devoted follower of Lord Ram, and he considered introducing himself as His devotee to be the best identification.

In Hindu society, people often introduce themselves by their caste, position, or wealth, which creates a negative atmosphere for them. A Hindu tradition still prevalent in Maharashtra is that people attach their father's name to their own name. We, who call ourselves Hindu and followers of Sanatan Dharma, should introduce ourselves like Hanuman. My introduction would be, "I am Anil Satish Chandra Srivastava, a devotee of Ram and follower of Sanatan Dharma."

When you identify yourself by your gods and elders, it eradicates arrogance. You will be surrounded by those who will keep you safe. Caste, religion, and social divisions are impurities of the Earth. Eliminate these and adopt the constitution established by the Ramayana, which teaches that your identity should be your God and revered ones. This practice will certainly eliminate the impurity of arrogance, which is leading humanity towards destruction and downfall.

****

CHAPTER - 56

Sunderkand

Doha: *Binay Na Maanat Jaladhi Jad Gaye Teen Din Beeti. Bole Ram Sakop Tab Bhay Bin Hoyi Na Preeti. (57)*

Meaning: When three days passed, and the obstinate ocean did not heed Ram's pleas, Ram angrily said that without fear, love does not arise.

Sanatan Dharmic Constitution: Appropriate Decision - Efforts of Dialogue and Persuasion:

The ocean knew that Lord Ram's wife had been abducted and that he was distressed and going to fight the demons, for which he needed a path. Instead of standing with dharma and giving way, the ocean remained uncooperative. It is necessary to end those who side with adharma, so Lord Ram took up his bow and said he would dry up the ocean with his arrows. Despite the ocean's stubbornness, Ram, being magnanimous, did not shoot his arrow immediately but only issued a warning. This gave the ocean a chance to stand with justice and correct its mistake. Ram could have dried up the ocean without any warning, but our Sanatan Dharma teaches us to give others a chance to rectify their errors before causing harm.

Ram's efforts were successful. The ocean admitted its mistake and apologized. It also requested that, instead of removing the water to create a path, Ram could take the help of Nala and Neel from his army. Nala and Neel were blessed and had the scientific knowledge to make stones float, allowing them to build a bridge without diminishing the ocean's honour.

Ram accepted this proposal. This reflects a Sanatan constitutional principle that before causing harm, one should explore all other options and engage in dialogue to find a solution. Today, nations and societies that resort to immediate violence, such as bombing and shooting, need to follow the Sanatan Dharmic constitution to ensure the survival of human civilization and avoid nature's wrath. The cries of adharma lead to nature's destruction.

This passage from the Ramayana teaches us that we should always strive to avoid causing harm and give others an opportunity to amend their mistakes. This approach promotes peace and justice, preventing unnecessary destruction and suffering.

****

CHAPTER - 57

Ayodhya Kand

Chhand: *Avadh Taha Jaha Ram Nivasu, Tahi Divasu Jaha Bhanu Prakasu.*

Meaning: Where Lord Ram resides, that is Ayodhya. Where the sunlight reaches, that is the day.

Sanatan Constitution: No place is inherently good or bad. Great people make a place good or bad.

To support Ram, Lakshman chose to accompany him to the forest for 14 years. When one has a great brother like Ram, even the forest is acceptable. Mother Sumitra willingly accepted her son's decision to go with Ram. She told Lakshman that where Ram is, that is Ayodhya. In our society, people visit pilgrimage sites where great people once were, but they don't think about becoming great themselves and creating new pilgrimage sites. Mother Sumitra says that where there is sunlight, there is day. The day is not a specific place; it is where the sunlight falls. These lines from the Ramayana contain profound wisdom. People need to spread light to illuminate greatness. Temples are not just for worship and vows; they remind us that someone great once came here. Every person should strive to become like that. It is better to suffer and follow dharma than to live in comfort with unrighteousness.

Here, another Sanatani constitution was created by Mother Sumitra. Instead of keeping her son in the palace, she sent him to the forest with his brother to fulfil his duty. A mother should prioritize family duty, i.e., social duty, over her own maternal love. Ram went to the forest on his father's orders, but Lakshman went voluntarily. His greatness has been underestimated in India, but in terms of duty, his sacrifice was immense and gave birth to the Sanatan constitution that one must always fulfil their duty to their elder brother.

Here, Ram himself created an example. His behaviour and sense of duty earned him immense love and respect from everyone at home and in the country. Everyone stood by Ram without any selfish motives. This happens only when a person is deeply devoted to dharma.

****

CHAPTER - 58

Hidden Great Facts Of Ramayana - The Great Bharat

Sanatan Constitution - The Leader is Not the Owner

The Ramcharitmanas contains numerous facts that have shaped the great Sanatan constitution, but people often overlook them. While Shri Ram is indeed the hero, the great personalities around him, influenced by his great character and the wisdom of his parents, have given rise to many other heroes. The Indian public has given importance to those who brought the most benefit, but not to those who were great in their sacrifice.

Bharat Ji, the brother of lord Ram was given the entire kingdom of Ayodhya without asking for it. He had all the comforts, the army, and fourteen years to establish himself as a great ruler. However, he renounced the comforts of the kingdom and took on the responsibilities of the state. He set up his place far from the palace in a small hut from where he managed the affairs of the kingdom. During the long fourteen years, he took care of the citizens just as Shri Ram would have.

Bharat Ji revered Shri Ram's sandals, placing them on his head and using them as a symbol of authority. He slept on the ground.

Shri Ram obeyed his father's command, but Bharat Ji voluntarily adhered to dharma and set an ideal example. Sacrifice is a sign of greatness. Great people establish new milestones of greatness; they are the heroes.

In the country, many worship Ram, but no one embodies Ram's character. No one adopts the greatness of Ram's brother Bharat. A nation and time become great when people perform great deeds and establish new milestones of greatness.

India's great civilization must maintain the tradition of greatness that began in Ram's era, so that this country can be recognized as a great Sanatani civilization.

****

CHAPTER - 59

Hidden Great Facts Of Ramayana - The Great Jatayu

Sanatani Constitution: Protecting Women is the Foremost Duty

If those who read the Ramayana understand its constitutional principles, which encompass both rules and duties, they would recognize that the protection of women is a duty for every being. Jatayu was a bird, and Ravana was the conqueror of the three worlds. Jatayu staunchly opposed Ravana's criminal act and fought against him. Jatayu knew he wouldn't win, but defending was a matter of dharma. The outcome was insignificant; what mattered was adhering to dharma.

In the Hindu civilization, this was the first instance of the violation of a woman's honour after the Satya Yuga, and Jatayu was the first being to fight for a woman's honour, setting an example that not only humans but also animals and birds should respect women and prevent their dishonour. If a bird could fight against the conqueror of the three worlds without fearing for his life, then it is the primary duty of humans to protect women. No matter how powerful the offender is, they will face the consequences of their actions.

Every police station in India should have an honoured portrait of Jatayu. This image would serve as a reminder that they are not lesser than a bird, and thus, there should be no disrespect toward women in their jurisdiction. Anyone who dares to dishonour a woman should be subject to punishment.

This principle from the Ramayana emphasizes that protecting women is a crucial duty and reflects the core values of Sanatan Dharma. Jatayu's selfless act of bravery is a timeless lesson in courage and righteousness for everyone.

****

CHAPTER - 60

Hidden Great Facts Of Ramayana – Every Effort Should Be Made To Avoid War

Sanatani Constitution: War Should Be Prevented Whenever Possible

Imagine the patience of a prince whose wife has been abducted. It takes six months to find her. Even when it is known who the abductor is, the prince suppresses all his anger and follows dharma. In wars, thousands of soldiers, who are not at fault, lose their lives. They fight for their country, even if their country is in the wrong. The families of those who die lose their loved ones—be it a son, husband, or brother.

Therefore, Lord Ram sent Angad , the son of Bali as an envoy to Ravana to negotiate peace and retrieve Mother Sita. Any other person would have declared war on the abductor from the first day, but Lord Ram came to establish the Sanatan Dharmic constitution. He followed dharma, set aside personal pain, and tried to prevent war.

Although war ultimately occurred because Ravana refused to return mother Sita, there was an honest attempt to prevent it. In today's world, leaders not only attack each other but also kill innocent civilians instead of fighting on the borders.

The time has come for India to show the world how protecting humanity is a ruler's primary duty. Once a life is lost, it cannot be brought back, so every effort should be made to prevent war and save lives.

Lord Ram's attempt to avoid war, even in the face of personal tragedy, exemplifies a fundamental principle of Sanatan Dharma: the preservation of life and peace. This lesson from the Ramayana underscores the importance of seeking peaceful solutions and protecting innocent lives, reminding leaders of their duty to humanity.

This principle from the Ramayana teaches that the first duty of a leader is to protect humanity and make every possible effort to prevent war, thereby saving lives and promoting peace.

****

CHAPTER - 61

Sanatan's Constitution: Utilize Power Not Misutilize Power

The Shri Ramcharitmanas contains two descriptions that demonstrate that no matter how powerful an evil person is, their downfall is inevitable. This is the constitution of Sanatan: power should be used to protect the good and the weak.

King Bali had received a boon from the gods that anyone who fought him would lose half of their strength to Bali. This meant that Bali would possess three-quarters of the combined strength, leaving his opponent with only a quarter, making it impossible for anyone to defeat him. Bali banished Sugriva and took away his royal rights, which might have been acceptable, but he committed a grave sin by making Sugriva's wife his own. This is why the gods sent Lord Ram to help, and Bali was killed. When Bali asked Lord Ram:

"I am the enemy and Sugriva is dear to you. What fault of mine, O Lord, caused you to kill me?"

In response, Lord Ram said that a younger brother's wife is like a daughter, and by forcibly marrying her, Bali committed a grave sin. Despite being mighty and powerful, Bali was killed due to his wrongdoing. None of the gods' blessings could save him.

Similarly, Ravana had nectar in his navel, making him invincible. However, by kidnapping Mother Sita, he committed a grave sin and was ultimately killed by Lord Ram, the conqueror of the three worlds. The gods' blessings are meant for good deeds; their misuse leads to one's downfall. This also sends a message from the gods that the disrespect of women is intolerable to them. Those guilty of dishonouring women will surely be punished.

The gods, whom we call deities, were people of a high civilization. Today, we humans are breaking the rules they established. If this does not stop, human civilization will be in danger. The new generation should follow the constitution described by the gods in the Ramayana, so that the Sanatan civilization can survive on Earth.

****

CHAPTER - 62

Hidden Great Facts Of The Ramayana – Nine Types Of Devotion Pleasing To Lord Shri Ram

Sanatan's Constitution: The Nine types of devotion

Lord Shri Ram went to Shabari's ashram in the forest to ask about the whereabouts of Mother Sita. The great Jatayu had advised Shri Ram to meet mother Shabari. Shabari was astonished to see Shri Ram and didn't know how to honour him as she wasn't a person of high deeds.

Shri Ram explained to Shabari that there are nine types of devotion, and he is pleased with any one of them. These nine types of devotion, as described by him, are the great constitution of Sanatan. Understanding the true meaning of these words and acting upon them is what pleases Shri Ram.

Pratham Bhakti Santanah Kar Sanga, Dusari Rati Mam Katha Prasanga

First Devotion: Association with saints. This means seeking the company of those who embody saintly behaviour and character. These are individuals whose conduct and virtues are exemplary, guiding others towards righteousness and fostering an environment where everyone can develop similar noble qualities.

Second Devotion: Love for my stories and discourses. This entails having a deep and genuine love for listening to and reflecting on the tales and teachings of the Lord. It indicates a sincere desire to connect with the divine through the narratives and lessons found in sacred texts, fostering a heartfelt relationship with God. Here it is necessary to understand the lord Shri Ram is not talking about him but he is talking about the character he adopted and the same should be adopted by other people also.

These two types of devotion emphasize the importance of good company and the love of divine stories, as they are crucial in nurturing one's spiritual growth and connection with the divine.

Gur Pad Pankaj Seva Teesri Bhakti Amaan

Chauthi Bhakti Mam Gun Gan Karai Kapata Taji Gaan

Third Devotion: Humble service to the lotus feet of the Guru. This means serving one's Guru with utmost humility and without any sense of pride. It involves dedicating oneself to the Guru, who is a source of knowledge and wisdom, and respecting and honouring them through selfless service.

Fourth Devotion: Singing the praises of Shri Ram's virtues without deceit. This devotion entails abandoning all forms of deceit and wholeheartedly singing and celebrating the virtues and qualities of Shri Ram. It means living a life that reflects the values and character of Shri Ram and renouncing all forms of hypocrisy and dishonesty.

These two types of devotion underscore the significance of humility and sincerity. Serving the Guru with humility and celebrating the divine qualities of Shri Ram without deceit are key aspects that endear one to the Lord.

Mantra Jap Mam Dridh Viswasa, Pancham Bhajan Si Ved Prakasa

Chhath Dam Sheel Birati Bahu Karma, Nirat Nirantar Sajjan Dharma

Fifth Devotion: Chanting my name with firm faith. Shri Ram greatly loves those who chant his name with unwavering faith. It is important to understand that Shri Ram is not just referring to chanting his own name, but also the names of Brahma, Vishnu, Mahesh, and the Supreme Brahman. This chanting signifies following the path shown by God and preparing oneself to meet the Supreme Father. This type of devotion is also described in the Vedas, which speak of the Supreme Brahman, not just Ram.

Sixth Devotion: Practicing self-control, cultivating good character, and engaging in many good deeds. This devotion involves controlling one's senses and building a virtuous character. It means renouncing worldly pleasures and adopting detachment, which is the path of the saints. Shri Ram is very affectionate towards such individuals and showers his grace upon them.

These two types of devotion highlight the importance of faith and discipline. Chanting the divine names with firm faith and leading a disciplined life with good character and self-control are essential aspects of devotion that please Shri Ram.

Saatvan Sam Mohi May Jag Dekha, Mote Sant Adhik Kari Lekha

Athvan Jathalabh Santosha, Sapanahun Nahin Dekhai Paradosha

Seventh Devotion: Seeing the entire world with an equal vision, as you see Shri Ram and as Shri Ram sees the whole world. This means loving all humans, serving them, helping them, and giving them the affection and respect that is accorded to saints. It emphasizes universal love and service.

Eighth Devotion: Being content with whatever one gets and not seeing the faults of others even in dreams, nor criticizing them. This devotion focuses on contentment and avoiding negativity towards others, even in thoughts or dreams.

Navam Saral Sab San Chhalhina, Mam Bharos Hiyan Harash Na Deena

Ninth Devotion: Simplicity and behaving without deceit with everyone, keeping faith in God, and neither being excessively joyful nor sorrowful in any situation. This devotion highlights honesty, simplicity, and maintaining a balanced emotional state, rooted in faith in God.

These devotions emphasize the importance of equality, contentment, and simplicity. Seeing everyone with equal regard, being content with what one has, avoiding criticism of others, and maintaining honesty and faith are crucial for pleasing Shri Ram.

If we compare these qualities of devotion to today's society, 80% of people are not eligible to be called truly alive. They will not receive God's devotion because they do not fully embody any of the nine paths of devotion.

Engaging in bad deeds and then frequently visiting temples is not a divine act. Humans should strive to fulfill not just one but all the mentioned forms of devotion.

To achieve true devotion and favor from God, one must:

Seek the company of the virtuous – Associate with those who exhibit saintly behavior and character.

Love and reflect on divine stories – Have a genuine love for the tales and teachings of the Lord.

Serve the Guru humbly – Serve one's Guru with utmost humility and without pride.

Sing praises without deceit – Abandon all forms of deceit and sincerely celebrate the virtues of the Lord.

Chant with firm faith – Chant the names of the divine with unwavering faith, signifying a commitment to the path shown by God.

Practice self-control and good character – Control one's senses, build virtuous character, and engage in good deeds.

See the world equally – View the entire world with an equal vision, loving and serving all humans.

Be content and avoid negativity – Be satisfied with whatever one receives and avoid criticizing others, even in thoughts.

Maintain simplicity and honesty – Live simply, behave without deceit, and keep faith in God, maintaining a balanced emotional state.

By embodying these principles, one aligns with the true spirit of devotion and divine grace, contributing to a righteous and harmonious society.

With more clarity Saints don't necessarily wear robes but possess saintly behaviour and character. Those who live with saints also develop saintly qualities, which benefit humanity and guide people towards the right path. The Lord himself is a seeker of true love. Those who communicate with God out of love, rather than selfishness, are very dear tohim. Singing praises of Shri Ram's qualities without deceit. This does not means praising Shri Ram, but means that those who follow Shri Ram's character and abandon deceit are dear to Ram. Serving the Guru who imparts knowledge is also pleasing to Shri Ram. Practicing self-control, virtuous conduct, and performing many good deeds. Shri Ram deeply loves those who chant his name (meaning Brahma, Vishnu, Mahesh, and the Supreme Brahma) and have firm faith. This chant means preparing oneself to follow the path shown by God and to meet the Supreme Father. This type of devotion is also mentioned in the Vedas, which talk about the Supreme Brahma, not just Ram. The is about controlling one's senses and building good character, renouncing worldly pleasures, and embracing the path of detachment, which is the way of saints. Such deeds make Shri Ram very affectionate towards them, and he showers his grace upon them. Seeing the whole world with an equal vision, as one would see Shri Ram, and as Shri Ram sees the entire world. This means loving all humans, serving them, helping them, and giving them the affection and respect of saints. Being content with whatever one gets and not seeing others' faults even in dreams, nor criticizing them. Simplicity and treating everyone without deceit, keeping faith in God, and neither feeling excessive joy nor sorrow in any situation. Shri Ram says that if any one of these nine types of devotion is found in anyone, they become eligible for God's grace, regardless of whether they are a man, woman, or any living being. It is important to note that even inanimate objects are considered alive. Air, water, fire, nature, trees, and plants are all living, and even they should possess some qualities of devotion.

****

CHAPTER - 63

Lanka Kand

Hidden Great Facts Of The Ramayana – All Radiant Light Merges Into The Divine:

Sanatan's Constitution: Your Radiance Is A Part Of The Divine

Verse: *"Tasu Tej Samaan Prabhu Aanana, Harashe Dekhi Sambhu Chaturanana."*

Meaning: Ravan's radiance merged into the Lord's mouth . Seeing this, Shiva and Brahma were delighted.

Sanatan's Constitution:

At the end of life, your radiance, i.e., your virtues, will merge into the Divine. When Ravan died, his body fell to the ground, but his radiance, which came from his virtuous and religious deeds, merged into Shri Ram's mouth. This clearly means that the radiance, or virtues, of every person ultimately merge into God. Shri Ram left Ravan's sins on the earth. The divine powers that had blessed Ravan were taken back because he was no longer worthy of them. Ravan misused these divine powers, and thus, God punished him with death and reclaimed the powers.

It is important to understand that when Ravan performed rituals, penances, and meditations, his virtuous deeds and devotion earned him great powers from the Divine. However, one cannot misuse the powers granted by God. When Ravan did so, the Lord punished him with death and reclaimed the powers he had granted.

The Ramayana contains infinite wisdom and constitutional principles that people should learn. The Ramayana is not just a story; it is a constitution. Each verse and word must be read carefully, understood for its purpose, and applied in life so that the followers of Sanatan Dharma can live on earth with the utmost humanity and love.

****

CHAPTER - 64

Hidden Great Facts Of The Ramayana - Arrows Returning To The Quiver:

Sanatan's Constitution: Reach For Divine Science

Verse: *"Prabise Sab Nishang Mahun Jai, Dekhi Suranha Dundubhi Bajai."*

Meaning: All the arrows returned to the quiver after hitting their targets. Seeing this, the gods sounded their drums in celebration.

Sanatan's Constitution:

The ancient science of Sanatan was far superior to today's science. The Ramayana conveys that in that era, there were such arrows that either destroyed the target and returned or were destroyed by the enemy if they were more powerful. The return of the arrows to the quiver signified that the target had been destroyed. It was a complete process: the target was aimed at, and if successful, the arrows returned to the quiver; if not, they were destroyed. This way, the archer could know the success or failure by whether the arrows returned or not. Similarly, the counter to an arrow was to destroy the opponent's arrow and then return to the quiver.

Another such scientific weapon is Shri Krishna's Sudarshan Chakra, which would hit or destroy the target and then return to him.

Modern science has not yet invented technology that allows us to use a weapon, have it destroy the target, and then return. It seems as if the arrows carried power in their tips, used it against the enemy, and then returned to gather new power.

Whatever the case, this verse from the Ramayana highlights our current scientific backwardness. The divine beings, whom we call gods, were masters of great science. Today, people go to temples to ask for this or that, but the truth is they have already given us a brain. We must use it to advance and benefit humanity.

****

CHAPTER - 65

Shri Ram Charit Manas - Mareech The Constitution Of Sanatan - Liberation Through Devotion To God.

Mareech was the uncle of Ravana. He was older than Ravana. After being born into the demon race and spending a long time in such a form, he became weary of the demonic nature. He started worshipping and performing penance for Lord Shiva. Pleased by this transformation, Lord Shiva blessed Mareech with salvation.

For Mareech's welfare and liberation from Earth, nature orchestrated a plan where Ravana approached him, and the conspiracy was devised for Mareech to become a golden deer to deceive Mother Sita. This was so that Lord Ram could personally liberate him from his demon life and grant him salvation.

We often wonder what was right and what was wrong. Why did Mother Sita desire the golden deer? Mother Sita ensured the direct path to heaven through her husband, Lord Ram. She neither had any longing nor did she desire anything. She had forsaken the kingdom of Ayodhya. Her kingdom was filled with gold, so how could she desire a golden deer?

The Constitution of Sanatan dictates that no matter how demonic a person's nature is, if they repent and take refuge in God, they will surely attain liberation. The episode of Mareech also demonstrates that nature works according to deeds. If someone is destined to meet God, nature ensures it happens.

Deeds are supreme. God rewards actions. This is stated in both Shri Ramcharit Manas and by Lord Vishnu when He incarnated as Lord Krishna in the Gita. Perform your duties without desiring the outcome, for only nature determines the reward of deeds. If nature can grant a demon salvation through God, it clearly conveys to humans that the proper reward for righteous deeds is certain.

****

CHAPTER - 66

Shri Ram Charit Manas - Angad And Vibhishan.

The Constitution of Sanatan - Living With Truth Means Living With Righteousness (Ram Dharma).

Angad was the son of Bali. His father was killed by Lord Ram in secrecy because Bali had a blessing that anyone who confronted him would lose half of their strength to Bali, making him invincible in battle. To end this injustice, Lord Ram took advantage of this situation, but under any circumstances, injustice had to be eradicated.

Angad accepted that his father was wrong. The wife of a younger brother Sugreev was like a daughter. Forcing her into marriage was a grave sin. Hence, Angad sided with Lord Ram. Lord Ram, fully respecting Angad, made him His emissary and sent him to Ravana's court, a task requiring great trust. Angad could have claimed the throne as the crown prince and could have even fought Sugriva if necessary, but he gave the throne to his father's brother and accepted Sugriva as the king because Sugriva was always on the side of righteousness. He had no greed for the throne. He only wanted to prove his innocence. He returned home only after a year of waiting for Bali's return. When he saw blood coming from cave and Bali not came out then he presumed the death of Bali and came back to country. The royal court offered him the throne; he did not seize it. Since Sugriva was on the side of truth and righteousness, Lord Ram supported him, and Angad supported Lord Ram. The clear message was always to stand with truth and righteousness. If one's father is unjust, even his support must be abandoned.

Similarly, shree Vibhishan abandoned his brother Ravana. Standing for righteousness, he was kicked and humiliated by Ravana and had to leave Lanka, but he renounced all the wealth because it was gained through unrighteous means. He sought refuge with Lord Ram. Because Vibhishan stood with righteousness, Lord Ram gave him the kingdom of Lanka. Vibhishan left his brother, wealth, and kingdom for the sake of righteousness, sending a clear message that those who stand with Lord Ram and righteousness should be supported by all righteous individuals.

These two episodes from Shri Ram Charit Manas establish the principle that no matter the relationship, no matter how close someone is, if they stand with unrighteousness, their support must be abandoned, and one should seek refuge in righteousness.

The ultimate results of standing with righteousness was Vibhishan became to king of Lanka and ruled for thousands of years. Similarly the Sugreeve got the kingdom of Kishkindha state. He made Angad is successor and a great respect as he was taking care of his brother Bali.

There may be delay in getting the justice because when you are with righteousness, you will be alone or very few will be with you but ultimately this universe will pay you everything for which you deserved. The treasure of happiness.

****

CHAPTER - 67

Shri Ram Charit Manas - Amrit

The Constitution of Sanatan - Even Amrit Cannot Save If Aligned With Adharma.

Shri Ram Charit Manas gives two messages regarding Amrit (nectar of immortality). First, that there exists an element, Amrit, on Earth that can grant immortality to any human. Ravana had Amrit in his navel. The navel is the center of the body and part of the umbilical cord, which nourishes a newborn and connects it to its mother. This connection to the mother signifies a link to the cosmic energy that sustains the child in the womb. Thus, there is a relationship between Amrit and this cosmic energy that can grant life and immortality. The mention of Amrit also occurs in the story of the churning of the ocean (Samudra Manthan). Therefore, it is established that the element Amrit exists on Earth. It is hidden in a manner similar to how coal, under extreme heat, transforms into a diamond, and Amrit is mixed with poison. Through churning, meaning extreme heat, they separate. This element grants immortality to humans, but if one stands with Adharma (unrighteousness) like Ravana, a proponent of Dharma can dry it up.

The Constitution of Sanatan is clear: Dharma (righteousness) and worthiness can grant immortality, while Adharma can dry up immortality. This means that the end of Adharma is certain. Creation has ordained a constitution where Adharma and evil must end. Any person aligned with Adharma will soon meet their end.

****

CHAPTER - 68

Shri Ram Charit Manas - Angad's Foot

Verse: *"Jo Mam Charan Sakasi Sath Taari, Phirahi Ramoo Sita Mai Haari."*

Meaning: Shri Angad said to Ravan, "O fool! If you can move my foot, Shri Ram will return to Ayodhya , and I will give up Mother Sita."

Sanatan's Constitution - Have Complete Faith in Yourself and the Power of Truth

Angad did not possess any blessing that made his foot immovable. Before him stood Ravan's immensely powerful warriors. So what made Angad confident enough to issue such a challenge, claiming that if his foot was moved, Shri Ram would return to Ayodhya and not take back Mother Sita? This significant challenge indicates Angad's complete confidence in his victory.

Angad had complete faith not only in his own strength but also in Shri Ram. This message is for the entire world: if you stand with truth, righteousness, respect for women, and the unwavering character of a saint, no evil force can move you. If your actions align with the path laid out by the gods, their power will be with you, providing the confidence for victory. Those aligned with evil will be inherently weak. They will be accompanied by arrogance, which only provides a momentary boost before making them vulnerable. An evil person's conscience and the knowledge of their wrongful acts weaken them from within.

Ravan and his court were aware, deep down, that their king had acted wrongfully. Their consciences reproached them. This is why they were defeated by Angad's radiance and Shri Ram's grace.

This also conveys a clear message: a good person, like Angad, should firmly plant their feet in truth, peace, and duty with all their might. There is no reason for truth to falter. Divine power is always with good people. Though unseen, it is present. No person who is pure, truthful, stands up for the weak, follows the path of righteousness, and upholds dharma is without the support of divine and cosmic forces. Invisible and indirect powers always support them.

****

CHAPTER - 69

Ayodhya Kanda

Verse: *"Pitu Surpur Ban Raghubar Ketu. Mai Keval Sab Anrath Hetu. Dhig Mohi Bhayu Benu Ban Aagi. Dusah Daah Dukh Dooshan Bhaagi."*

Meaning: "Father is in heaven, and Shri Ram is in the forest. I am solely the cause of all these misfortunes, like the comet (Ketuke). Shame on me, as I am like the fire in a bamboo forest, bringing unbearable pain, suffering, and blame."

Doha: *"Maatu Bharat Ke Bachan Mradu Suni Puni Uthi Sambhaari. Liye Uthai Lagaai Ur Lochan Mochati Baari."*

Meaning: "Upon hearing Bharat's gentle words, Mother Kausalya rose up again, took Bharat in her arms, embraced him, and tears flowed from her eyes."

Sanatan's Constitution - One should judge and respect a person based on their character. The human values are more important than kingdom and personal profit or loss

When Bharat returned to Ayodhya, he was shocked to learn of the grave misdeed his mother had committed in such a short time. His father had passed away in grief, and his elder brother, along with his wife and younger brother, had gone to the forest. He realized that he was the cause of all this because his mother, Kaikeyi, had asked for the three boons to give her son Bharat the throne. Bharat, being just and honourable, refused the throne. He went to Mother Kausalya and said that he was the cause of all these misfortunes.

Hearing Bharat's gentle and truthful words, Mother Kausalya embraced him and wept. This significant message in Shri Ram Charit Manas teaches that respect should be given based on a person's character. Mother Kausalya did not think that Bharat had any ill intentions or that his mother had done everything for him, causing her son to go to the forest and her husband to pass away. She listened to Bharat's truthful words, understood them, and gave him the same maternal love as before. There was no ill will in her heart towards Bharat despite the suffering caused to her husband and son because of him. People remarked that she was indeed the mother of Shri Ram, possessing such a noble personality.

Mother Kausalya explained to Bharat that everything was the will of destiny and God. Whatever is meant to happen will happen. Do not blame anyone. You are dearly loved by Shri Ram himself.

This incident showcases numerous examples of greatness. Bharat was not happy to receive the throne, and Mother Kausalya attributed the misfortunes to fate, maintaining her love and justice for her children at the highest level. They prioritized human values over material wealth. Bharat rejected the throne.

If we reflect on this event, it emphasizes greatness at every turn. Bharat was not joyful about receiving the throne, and Mother Kausalya blamed fate while upholding her maternal love and sense of justice at the highest level. They valued human principles over material comfort. Bharat rejected the throne.

Now, for those who claim to follow Sanatan Dharma, do they adhere to these human values? To follow Sanatan Dharma means to abide by the constitutional principles given in Shri Ram Charit Manas.

****

CHAPTER - 70

Lanka Kanda Prahastha

Sanatan's Constitution: Do not stand with or support injustice.

Doha: *"Sab Ke Bachan Shravan Suni Kah Prahastha Kar Jori. Neeti Virodh Na Kariya Prabhu Mantrinah Mati Ati Thori."*

Meaning: After hearing the unjust words of the ministers in the court, Prahastha folded his hands and said to Ravana, "O Lord, we should not act against justice. The ministers have very little wisdom."

Prahastha further explained, "If you can devour the monkeys, why didn't you devour Hanuman, who set the whole of Lanka on fire and left? The Rama who built a bridge over the sea and came with his army to Suvela Mountain is not a mere human whom we can simply devour. I am not a coward. I oppose acting against justice. Speaking sweet words in front of you does not benefit the king or the subjects. If Rama retrieves his wife and leaves, we should not escalate the conflict."

However, it is the divine law that when evil is destined to end, God corrupts their intellect. They cannot distinguish between truth and falsehood. Under the influence of this delusion, Ravana harshly replied to Prahastha:

***Verse:** "Abhi Te Ur Sansay Hoi. Benumul Sut Bhayahu Ghamoi. Suni Pitu Gira Parush Ati Ghora. Chala Bhavan Kahi Bachan Kathora."*

Meaning: "Do you have doubts or fears in your heart already? Son, you have turned out to be like a weed growing in a bamboo grove." Hearing his father's extremely harsh and bitter words, Prahastha left for his home, saying that just as medicine does not seem pleasant to a patient nearing death, good advice is not welcomed by those close to their doom.

People often do not know the story of Prahastha. To make Ravana understand, the names of Hanuman, Angad, Vibhishana, and Mandodari are usually mentioned. However, Ravana's son Prahastha also deserves the same respect because he too opposed injustice.

****

CHAPTER - 71

Aranya Kand

Sanatan's Constitution: Protecting the Honor of Women - The Supreme Duty that Leads to Heaven.

Verse: *"Those who have the welfare of others in their hearts, for them nothing is unattainable in this world. O dear one! Leave your body and come to my supreme abode. What can I give you? You are already fulfilled."*

Meaning: Those whose hearts are dedicated to the welfare of others find nothing in this world unattainable. O dear one! Leave your body and come to my supreme abode. What can I offer you? You are already fully accomplished.

Doha: *"O dear one, do not speak to our father about the abduction of Sita. If I am truly Ram, then the ten-headed Ravana will come and confess to our family himself."*

Meaning: O dear one, do not tell our father about Sita's abduction. If I am truly Ram, then the ten-headed Ravana will come and admit it to the family himself.

Verse: *"Jatayu, having left his vulture form, assumed a divine form, adorned with numerous exquisite ornaments and a beautiful yellow garment. His body was dark, with four large arms. He praised the Lord with eyes filled with tears of joy."*

Meaning: Jatayu left his vulture form and took on a divine form, adorned with numerous exquisite ornaments and a beautiful yellow garment. His body was dark, with four large arms, and with eyes filled with tears of joy, he praised the Lord.

Explanation:

Much has been conveyed here. A constitution has been established. Even among birds, the vulture is a fierce carnivore. Its life was not virtuous, implying it still had many births left to take in various animal and bird forms. However, it followed its duty. It fought against the mighty Ravana to protect Mother Sita, without caring for its own life. It risked its life for the sake of righteousness. For this noble act of protecting a woman's honor, Lord Ram sent it directly to the supreme abode of God. Freeing it from the cycle of birth and death, granting it a life free from suffering. Jatayu left his vulture form, attained a divine form, and was ready to proceed to the Lord's abode when Lord Ram instructed him not to tell Dasharatha about Sita's abduction. He would be grieved. If he truly belonged to Dasharatha's lineage, Ravana would come himself with his family and confess. This implied that Ravana and his family would meet their end, but since they would die at the hands of a divine being, they too would attain heaven and speak about their actions and the consequences they faced.

This description is very significant as it establishes that it is every human's duty to protect and honor women. Those who fail to do so meet their demise. Those who uphold women's honor are always dear to God and attain the divine abode. In today's dark age of Kali Yuga, every human should read the Ramayana and follow the constitution laid out in it. The gods themselves created and followed this constitution.

In the context of the Ramayana, it is also made clear that there are numerous realms where God resides. There is no sorrow there, and life is eternal. A person who performs good deeds, remains in contact with God, and follows divine devotion can be freed from the cycle of birth and death and attain God. The question people ask today about the existence of life on other planets has already been answered in our Vedas and other religious texts. There are countless realms and infinite beings in this universe. Even within our Milky Way galaxy, there is a planet called Dhava where human life exists. Reading and following the facts presented in the Ramayana and the Vedas is the foremost duty of a human being.

****

CHAPTER - 72

Shri Ram Charit Manas - The Truth Behind The Desire For The Golden Deer

Verse: *Seeing his death inevitable in both ways, Maricha sought refuge in Raghunath Ji.*
"Answering or not answering, this unfortunate one will kill me. So why not die by being struck by Raghupati's arrow?"

Meaning: When Maricha saw his death as certain in both scenarios, he considered it proper to take refuge in Shri Raghunath Ji. Maricha thought, "If I refuse, this unfortunate Ravana will kill me anyway. So why not die by being struck by Shri Raghunath Ji's arrow?"

Verse: *Sita saw the extremely beautiful deer, each part of its body was very enchanting.*
"Listen, O merciful Raghuveer, this deer has a very beautiful skin."

Meaning: Sita Ji saw that extremely beautiful deer, each part of its body was extremely enchanting. Sita Ji said, "O Lord! O merciful Raghuveer, please listen, this deer has very beautiful skin."

Verse: *"O truthful Lord, please catch it for me," said Vaidehi. Then Raghupati, knowing all the reasons, got up happily to accomplish the gods' work.*

Meaning: "O truthful Lord, please catch it for me," said Sita (Vaidehi). Then Raghupati (Shri Ram), knowing all the reasons, happily got up to accomplish the gods' work.

The Eternal Constitution - Even if a sinner, whether a demon or anyone else, becomes a devotee of the Lord, he attains heaven.

When Ravana pressured Maricha to deceitfully become a golden deer to lure Ram into the forest so that he could abduct Sita, Maricha understood that if he refused, Ravana would kill him. It was better to be killed by Shri Ram's arrow. Dying at Shri Ram's hands would lead to salvation.

Actually, despite being from a demon clan, Maricha became a devotee of Lord Shiva and started meditating on God. He had renounced all demonic tendencies. Thus, being a great devotee of Shiva, he was destined for salvation, and Ravana's end was also certain. The Supreme Father made arrangements for this.

Sita Ji expressed her desire for the golden deer's skin upon seeing it. It is important to understand that Mother Sita, who was the daughter of Earth and the caretaker of all beings, wanted the deer's skin. Someone whose father's and husband's houses were filled with gold and who lived in a palace adorned with gold, why would she want the skin of a golden deer? She was living by consuming roots and fruits. Mother Sita did not send Lakshman because Maricha could only attain the divine abode and salvation from Shri Ram.

Therefore, the divine play, based on karma, led Maricha to the divine abode through Lord Vishnu himself. Ravana, who was a devotee of Shiva, incurred the sin of killing a devotee of Shiva, ensuring his own death.

The constitution of Sanatan Dharma established through this episode is that no matter how much of a devotee of Shiva someone is and how blessed they are, if they engage in unrighteousness and deceit, their end is determined by nature itself. Similarly, if an unrighteous person follows the path of righteousness, God grants them shelter in the divine abode. Therefore, every being should practice devotion to God and follow the path laid out in the Ramayana and other scriptures of Sanatan Dharma.

****

Message From Author And Co-Author

Entertainment is necessary, and for that, we have various resources like social media and movies. However, serious guidance for life is found only in books. The books we study in classrooms provide us with knowledge to secure good jobs, but they often fall short in offering logical solutions to real-life problems.

Today's youth often hesitate to seek clarity from their parents. Instead, they turn to friends, many of whom unintentionally misguide them. Therefore, it is essential to create **libraries on every street**, where our youth can access valuable knowledge and learn how to live meaningful and principled lives.

Unfortunately, modern business practices have altered the moral **compass**. Bribery is now considered a part of daily life rather than a crime. Breaking the law is often justified as a necessity for business survival. Meanwhile, inappropriate language and content have entered our bedrooms through television and streaming platforms. The question arises—who is guiding our youth on the right path?

This book is an attempt to provide that guidance. We encourage young people to start spending more time in libraries. Movies and shows often carry disclaimers, saying "this is a work of fiction." But books written by thoughtful authors do not need such disclaimers—they convey truth and wisdom.

Join our mission: **Gift a Book**—and help make India the most educated country in the world.

Author - A. K. Srivastava
Co-Author - Akshay Srivastava